Essential Guides for
EARLY CAREER
TEACHERS

Understanding Your Role in Curriculum Design and Implementation

Essential Guides for Early Career Teachers

The *Essential Guides for Early Career Teachers* provide accessible, carefully researched, quick-reads for early career teachers, covering the key topics you will encounter during your training year and first two years of teaching. They complement and are fully in line with the new *Early Career Framework* and are intended to assist ongoing professional development by bringing together current information and thinking on each area in one convenient place. The texts are edited by Emma Hollis, Executive Director of the National Association of School-Based Teacher Trainers (NASBTT), who brings a wealth of experience, expertise and knowledge to the series.

Why not explore the other books in this series?

Essential Guides for
EARLY CAREER
TEACHERS

Understanding Your Role in Curriculum Design and Implementation

NASBTT

Henry Sauntson
Series editor: Emma Hollis

First published in 2023 by Critical Publishing Ltd

British Library Cataloguing in Publication Data
A CIP record for this book is available from the British Library

ISBN: 978-1-915080-65-3

This book is also available in the following e-book formats:

EPUB ISBN: 978-1-915080-66-0
Adobe e-book ISBN: 978-1-915080-67-7

The right of Henry Sauntson to be identified as the author of this work has been asserted by him in accordance with the Copyright, Design and Patents Act 1988.

Cover and text design by Out of House Limited
Project management by Newgen Publishing UK
Printed and bound in Great Britain by 4edge, Essex

Critical Publishing
3 Connaught Road
St Albans
AL3 5RX

www.criticalpublishing.com

Printed on FSC accredited paper

To order our books please go to our website www.criticalpublishing.com or contact our distributor Ingram Publisher Services, telephone 01752 202301 or email IPSUK.orders@ingramcontent.com. Details of bulk order discounts can be found at www.criticalpublishing.com/delivery-information.

Our titles are also available in electronic format: for individual use via our website and for libraries and other institutions from all the major ebook platforms.

Contents

Meet the series editor

Emma Hollis

I am Executive Director of the National Association of School-Based Teacher Trainers (NASBTT) and my absolute passion is teacher education. After gaining a first-class degree in psychology, I trained as a primary teacher and soon became head of initial teacher education for a School-Centred Initial Teacher Training (SCITT) provider. I see teacher education as a continuum and, while my heart will always be very close to the initial stages of a teacher's development, I am also dedicated to ensuring that teachers are given access to high-quality professional development throughout their careers.

Meet the author

Henry Sauntson

I gained a PGCE in English and media and have since worked in various roles in middle and senior leadership. I took over as director of a SCITT in the East of England after working with it as a lead mentor and have dedicated myself to raising the profile and quality of initial teacher education in this region and across wider networks. I believe in the power of high-quality teacher education and recognise the positive impact effective teachers can have on educational outcomes for students.

Acknowledgements

Fully understanding all the complexities of curriculum can be a challenge. Like the fabled painting of the Forth Road Bridge, it is never complete, as curriculum is ever-changing. Arguments abound, theories are posited, approaches are contested, but it has been lovely – during the course of putting together this book – to learn more about it myself. As teachers and educators, we must never stop learning lest we stagnate – that should be motive enough for us all.

To my wonderful wife, Sarah, and my three wonderful children, Mary, Agatha and Rowan – who will be excited to see their names in a 'real book' – thank you for your time and support, always.

To all those whose work I have cited, referenced or simply admired herein – thank you.

I am grateful always to those who give me the opportunity to develop as a professional and also share my thinking – without their belief, this book might not be here.

Thank you also to the staff and students at Arthur Mellows Village College, and to the trainees and staff at the Teach East SCITT, which I am very lucky to be able to lead.

Finally, thank you to Emma Hollis (NASBTT) for her superb critical eye and for keeping my language on the ground as opposed to off in wild flights of fancy, and to Julia and Lily at Critical Publishing for offering me advice, setting deadlines and then being forgiving when I missed them.

I do hope this book is of use to those entering the profession and those within it, and especially those who support others as they begin their teaching journey. As teacher educators, we give back because we appreciate what we ourselves received.

Craft is what enables you to be successful when you are not inspired.

Brian Eno

Foreword

As a passionate advocate of high-quality teacher education and continuing professional development (CPD), it has always been a source of frustration to me that beyond the Initial Teacher Education (ITE) year, access to high-quality, structured, ongoing professional development has been something of a lottery for teachers. Access and support has been patchy, with some schools and local authorities offering fantastic opportunities for teachers throughout their careers while in other locations CPD has been given lip service at best and is sometimes non-existent.

This series was conceived to attempt to close some of those gaps and to offer accessible professional learning to busy teachers in the early stages of their careers. It was therefore a moment of genuine pleasure when proposals for an entitlement for all early career teachers (ECTs) to receive a package of support, guidance and education landed on my desk. Through the Early Career Framework, there is now a genuine opportunity for school communities to work together to offer the very best early career development for our most precious of resources: the teachers in our schools.

The aim of this series is to distil some of the key topics that occupy the thoughts of ECTs into digestible, informative texts that will promote discussion, contemplation and reflection, and will spark further exploration into practice. In each volume, you will find a series of practical suggestions for how you can put the big idea in each chapter into practice: now, next week and in the long term. By offering opportunities to bring the learning into the classroom in a very concrete way, we hope to help embed many of the principles we share into your day-to-day teaching lives.

In this book, Henry Sauntson reminds us that all teachers are curriculum curators, designers and facilitators. As an ECT, it may be tempting to see the curriculum as something that is written by others and delivered by you in the classroom. Yet, as Henry points out, it is only through the teacher that a curriculum truly comes alive. Even if you are working from a published scheme of work, the decisions you make about where to add emphasis, the anecdotes and metaphors you draw on to exemplify a concept and the aspects you choose to focus on most and least are all vital facets of curriculum design. In this book, you are offered practical and actionable ways to think about yourself in this role and to ensure that the pupils you teach get the very best version of the curriculum with which you are working.

Emma Hollis,
Executive Director, NASBTT

Chapter 1   Introduction: what is curriculum?

The teacher, like the artist, the philosopher and the man of letters, can only perform his work adequately if he feels himself to be an individual directed by an inner creative impulse, not dominated and fettered by an outside authority.
(Bertrand Russell, 1961, p 420)

Introduction

Curriculum isn't just written – that's far too passive. Curriculum is made, sculpted, enacted: in the same way that a playwright manufactures their scripts as three-dimensional, living constructs (hence 'wright' as opposed to 'write'), so a teacher breathes life into a curriculum through their classroom and the wider vision of the school.

The Early Career Framework (Department for Education, 2019a) sets out, in Standard 3, the following 'Learn That' statement:

> *A school's curriculum enables it to set out its vision for the knowledge, skills and values that its pupils will learn, encompassing the national curriculum within a coherent wider vision for successful learning.*

It is an essential part of every teacher's knowledge base – their ability to make professional decisions informed by a clear understanding of the principles and implications of their choice. Curriculum is a huge part of every pupil's education – it is the map of their journey: what they will learn, when and, as we explore later, how they will learn it. In order to make good decisions, we use a combination of pedagogical knowledge and practice wisdom – we need to make these decisions on the basis of clear evidence.

This introductory chapter looks at what curriculum is, why it is important and what it means to you. Subsequent chapters then delve further into each element, developing your knowledge base and providing you with tasks and opportunities for reflection.

Many a debate rages around the role, purpose, intention and foundation of 'curriculum' and, as an early career teacher (ECT), you will hear the term used in a range of circumstances and scenarios. As curriculum is only actively realised in classrooms, you play a big role in its success, so it is vital that you understand not only some of the more recognised theories but also the design principles and intent, the way curriculum can be implemented and the impact it can have, as well as how to evaluate curriculum for continued improvement.

As the world enters the post-Covid-19 era, and society starts to truly acknowledge the enormity of the impact of the pandemic and the enforced partial closures of school settings, we begin to see also just how powerful a tool a well-crafted, considerate and equitable curriculum really is in ensuring the future success and efficacy of our pupils.

This book doesn't contain all the answers, nor does it raise all the questions; however, it does hope to provide you with insight into why curriculum matters to you and what you can do to understand, use and develop it effectively.

What? (The big idea)

What is curriculum? Why does curriculum matter? You can find a wealth of research, evidence and experience related to curriculum, and can see it defined, redefined and mis-defined across a veritable smorgasbord of publications and opinion pieces. However, one thing that must be agreed upon is how integral curriculum is to the successful education and development of pupils, and the need for all teachers of all levels of experience across all key stages to understand their role in its intent, implementation and impact. We explore each of these areas in greater depth in the course of this book. Brophy (2000, p 14) puts it nicely:

> A curriculum is not an end in itself; it is a means of helping students to learn what is considered essential for preparing them to fulfil adult roles in society and realise their potential as individuals. Its goals are learner outcomes – the knowledge, skills, attitudes, values and dispositions to action that society wishes to develop in its citizens.

One thing you can be sure of is that curriculum is not just a catch-all term for a whole-school programme of study. Yes, there is the national curriculum but every lesson taught in every school every day of the academic year is a constituent part of one or more curricula – it is a concept that is made concrete by its enactment on a daily basis to further pupil outcomes. Dylan Wiliam (2013, p 10) tells us that curriculum is *'the lived daily experience of young people in classrooms ... curriculum is pedagogy'*.

In simple terms, curriculum can be viewed as the vehicle by which knowledge is transferred from teacher to pupil – the way it is received, absorbed, grappled with. It is a marriage of intent, content, cognition and culture – every teacher brings something to curriculum and it has multiple aspects. It is the master of assessment, not its servant – assessment helps to validate and inform the taught curriculum; curriculum is the manna on which students feast, and assessment determines how well they have digested it.

The national curriculum in England

The national curriculum is statutory – it is issued by law and must be followed unless there is a good reason not to do so. However, it is only statutory for schools that are maintained by local authorities. Academies are not bound by it, but largely meet its detailed entitlements. The national curriculum sets out the *'programmes of study and attainment targets for all subjects'* across Key Stages 1 to 4, from Reception to the General Certificate of Secondary Education (GCSE). It has been in existence in its current form since 2014 (Department for Education, 2014), with English and mathematics updates in 2016 (Department for Education, 2016).

The introduction to the document states:

> *Every state-funded school must offer a curriculum which is balanced and broadly based and which promotes the spiritual, moral, cultural, mental and physical development of pupils at the school and of society, and prepares pupils at the school for the opportunities, responsibilities and experiences of later life.*
> (Department for Education, 2016, p 5)

The aims of the national curriculum are also worth noting:

> *The national curriculum provides pupils with an introduction to the essential knowledge that they need to be educated citizens. It introduces pupils to the best that has been thought and said; and helps engender an appreciation of human creativity and achievement.*
> (Department for Education, 2016, p 6)

Yet the national curriculum is just one aspect of the whole education of every child in the school system. Although teachers can feel pressured at times, with sensible planning and efficient pedagogy there is space and time in any academic year to go outside the bounds of what the national curriculum specifies. If you use the national curriculum as the outline of core knowledge in each subject discipline, you can create and deliver engaging and stimulating learning experiences for your pupils, promoting not only their academic prowess in each aspect of the curriculum, but also their social, emotional and mental development as part of a wider approach.

So what? ◀ ◀ ◀

If curriculum is indeed pedagogy, then the teacher as the pedagogue is the bearer of the curriculum banner. Every teaching decision you make, every lesson you plan, every sequence you design, every task you scaffold, every question you ask and every response you assess forms part of the big picture of curriculum. It goes almost without saying, then, that you have a huge responsibility to understand not only the rudiments of curriculum design but also the way it is enacted, implemented and measured in school settings – you have a duty to realise the curriculum, to manifest it. You will hopefully be there at its inception, facilitate its gestation and give birth to it in the classroom – and you can't do that if you don't know what you are doing or, worse still, why you are doing it.

Curriculum design is a fascinating and contentious topic, rich with debate and ripe with conflict. It is very easy to get submerged in the waters of research, to get lost down the rabbit holes of concepts and theories, but the main purpose of any good curriculum is to develop, strengthen and consolidate knowledge. It is there to be remembered. If nothing is remembered or retained, then nothing has been taught – the curriculum was flawed. All curriculum models have their contexts, and all contexts have their curriculum models – the very nature of education is that one size fits very few.

There can be curricula for behaviour or for professional development; the concern of this book is the curriculum of the classroom – the transfer of knowledge from teacher to pupil to facilitate the development of expertise, to promote mastery, to produce rounded and competent individuals capable of functioning successfully in the modern world.

Successful curriculum design depends so much on its implementation and its impact, and on the criteria against which these are measured: *'every system is perfectly designed to get the results it gets'* – a phrase attributed to a number of people, including W Edwards Deming (The Deming Institute, 2023). There are multiple interacting and conflicting variables, numerous logistical hurdles and many a slip from cup to lip – there are traditionalists, progressives, conformists, constructivists, functionalists, romantic radicals and scholarly structuralists; there are those who favour knowledge over skill, those who advocate starting with the child and those who posit the adult as the desired outcome. There are also those who seek to bank, feed, sculpt and emancipate; curriculum is contentious, but the contention arrives largely through the way it is interpreted and perceived. You cannot fall solely into one curriculum camp and remain there – curriculum development is a product of historical development, but if a curriculum is scrutinised purely as a product of a particular historical period, it is done a disservice. You do not exist in neatly packaged and ordered chronological packages – you are always learning, always adapting, always developing. Curriculum is organic. It is responsive. It is what happens in your classrooms. It is teaching.

So, whether you are a Key Stage 1 phonics specialist or a GCSE drama teacher, you *are* the embodiment of curriculum delivery – you need to know your stuff.

Reflective task ◀◀◀

The best reflection is guided by the boundaries of the known; you cannot reflect on things you don't understand or that haven't happened. So a starting point for reflection should be your own experience so far – your own teaching. Begin with the following questions.

- How well do you know your current curriculum?

- What are the principles on which it is built?

- What is its core content?

- Why are you teaching a particular topic or a particular skill at that particular time?

Now what?

If, as we have determined, the individual teacher is such an intrinsic part of curriculum, then the individual teacher must be prepared to have that impact – they must know the core principles, the research and evidence, the intent, the strategies for implementation, the desired outcomes and impact, and the cycle of evaluation and reflection that accompanies a curriculum. Nothing in education is in isolation; every decision or intervention is only as good as what preceded it and what follows it. If the main goal of any curriculum is the efficient, effective and timely transfer of knowledge and skills to build schema in long-term memory, then as enactors of the curriculum you must be confident in the terms used, the theories referenced and the breadth of available strategies for implementation.

A good basis for initial exploration of the importance of curriculum is through the Core Content Framework (Department for Education, 2019b), and the mentions of curriculum therein.

For example, those in Initial Teacher Education (ITE) are entitled to '*Learn how to ... deliver a carefully sequenced and coherent curriculum by ...* (author's choice of emboldened phrases):

> » *Receiving clear, consistent and effective mentoring in how to identify* ***essential concepts, knowledge, skills and principles of the subject***.

>> *Observing how expert colleagues ensure pupils' thinking is focused on* **key ideas within the subject** *and deconstructing this approach.*

>> *Discussing and analysing with expert colleagues the* **rationale for curriculum choices**, *the process for arriving at current curriculum choices, and how the school's* **curriculum materials inform lesson preparation**.

(Department for Education, 2019b)

The groundwork is laid – in this definition, curriculum can be seen to be the overarching journey of the pupil through a specific topic or unit of work, acquiring skills and knowledge en route. Further down the list, the statements are references to mastery, modelling, aligned resources, misconceptions, mental models, revisiting big ideas (Chapter 6), linking new content to core concepts, retrieval, spaced practice, recall, interleaving, critical thinking – it's a big list.

At the end of the journey, the curriculum can then be evaluated, ready for the next cycle; you can learn to consider the intent, content, delivery and lived experience of the curriculum through the eyes of your students and yourself as a classroom practitioner.

Reflective task ◀◀◀

In their recent book *How Teaching Happens*, Kirschner et al (2022, p 19) refer to curricular knowledge as:

Knowledge of the full range of how to teach the content at a certain level, the instructional materials available, and when, why, and how to use or not use certain things in certain circumstances.

This is a mighty definition, and one that is difficult to comprehend in its entirety for a teacher at any level of experience. You have to see yourself as a part of a whole. In the same way as each individual lesson contributes to a bigger picture of learning, so too each individual teacher contributes to a bigger picture of implementation.

- How confident do you currently feel about your role in the curriculum? Elaborate on your answer.

Practical task for tomorrow ◀◀◀

Choose one topic that you are currently teaching. Look carefully at a copy of the long-term scheme of learning for it and see whether you can break it into small steps – not individual lessons.

- How does each step build on the learning from the previous steps?

- How long should each step take?

- What is the final destination?

- Does the planned coverage time match the time available on the timetable?

Practical task for next week ◀◀◀

Let's refer back to the Core Content Framework (CCF) statements from earlier in this chapter. For the topic you chose for the previous task, answer these questions.

- What are the *essential concepts, knowledge, skills and principles of the subject?*

- What are the *key ideas within the subject?*

- What is the *rationale for this curriculum choice?*

- What are the available *curriculum materials* you can tap into?

Practical task for the longer term ◀◀◀

Keep a curriculum diary for each of your topics this year – this may simply be your planner, or a more detailed document.

Keep track of your answers to the following questions.

- Was the necessary prior knowledge in place with pupils before commencing the unit?

- What gaps are you filling or what concepts are you developing with regard to teaching?

- Are you succeeding in covering the intended content in the time available?

- What choices are you making about what to include and what to omit?

- What pedagogical approaches are you choosing to match the tasks and instruction set out in the planning document?

- How are you ensuring that all pupils have equitable access to the curriculum?

- What changes would you make if you taught this part of the curriculum again?

What next? ◀ ◀ ◀

Further reading

The National Curriculum: There is no better place to start than with the statutory requirements for curriculum content, which can be found at www.gov.uk/government/collections/ national-curriculum. This framework contains the specific content required for each subject and at each Key Stage, and you should make yourself familiar with it.

References

Brophy, J (2000) *Teaching; Educational Practice Series 1*. Geneva: UNESCO IBE.

The Deming Institute (2023) Deming Quotes. [online] Available at: https://deming.org/quotes/10141 (accessed 15 February 2023).

Department for Education (2014) *The National Curriculum in England – Framework Document*. [online] Available at: https://assets.publishing.service.gov.uk/government/uploads/system/uploads/attachment_data/file/381344/Master_final_national_curriculum_28_Nov.pdf (accessed 14 February 2023).

Department for Education (2016) *National Curriculum in England: Framework for Key Stages 1 to 4*. [online] Available at: www.gov.uk/government/publications/national-curriculum-in-england-framework-for-key-stages-1-to-4 (accessed 14 February 2023).

Department for Education (2019a) *Early Career Framework*. [online] Available at: https://assets.publishing.service.gov.uk/government/uploads/system/uploads/attachment_data/file/978 358/Early-Career_Framework April_2021.pdf (accessed 15 February 2023).

Department for Education (2019b) *Initial Teacher Training – Core Content Framework*. [online] Available at: https://assets.publishing.service.gov.uk/government/uploads/system/uploads/attachment_data/file/974307/ITT_core_content_framework_.pdf (accessed 14 February 2023).

Kirschner, P, Heal, J and Hendrick, C (2022) *How Teaching Happens*. London: Routledge.

Russell, B (1961) *The Basic Writings of Bertrand Russell.* London: Routledge.

Wiliam, D (2013) *Principled Curriculum Design*. London: SSAT.

Chapter 2   The journey so far

The most important single factor influencing learning is what the learner already knows. Ascertain this and teach accordingly.

(Ausubel, 1968, np)

Introduction

When I was young – in the days before navigation apps – it was my mother's duty (as the passenger, never the driver) to navigate on longer car journeys. Routes were planned and pored over prior to departure; Automobile Association (AA) road maps were like catnip to my father and any relative who cared to listen. It was often a key point of discussion at any family gathering – *'Which way did you come?'* or *'Which way are you going back?'* There would be debate, of course, and subjective opinion and preference – everyone had a favoured route and a reason for it. On those journeys, my mother had to make the right calls at the right time, and there was inherent shame in stopping and asking for directions. In fact, one my father's favourite responses to anyone who asked him directions to anywhere would be the deliberately pithy and confusing *'well, I wouldn't start from here'*. Imagine if that were a pupil asking you where they were going, what they were doing or how to get there? Imagine, worse still, if you couldn't provide an answer. Maybe that's curriculum right there – just as both the planning and discussion with the AA road map or the reliance on navigation apps require knowledge of the final destination, the possible pitfalls and choke-points along the way, and the outside chance of a diversion or a re-route to avoid unknown areas. As a teacher, to continue the analogy, you are both my mother and my father: you know the destination, you have an idea of the best route, you have a rough estimate of your arrival time and, more importantly, you're also driving the car – the classroom. You are the navigation app for your pupils on their 'learning journey' – so no pressure.

What? (The big idea)

The root of curriculum

What is the root of curriculum? For most adults under 40, their school experiences were determined by the national curriculum that was introduced nationwide for state schools in 1988 following the Education Reform Act. Prior to this, curricula were determined by local authorities or schools themselves, meaning great diversity in offer and approach. The concept of a 'core curriculum of basic knowledge' was first outlined by Sir Jim Callaghan in 1976, but it wasn't until 12 years later that it came to fruition. Schools were faced with the challenge of combining subjects to be studied with final examination preparation and enrichment opportunities, maximising potential for pupils and not limiting access to knowledge, but also delivering that knowledge in the most efficient way.

It must be remembered that the national curriculum in England does not apply to academies or free schools, but should still represent a touchstone; since 1988, there have been myriad reforms and reworkings of the national curriculum – content, assessment, subjects and so on – but the current iteration of the national curriculum acts as an outline, a framework.

If we see the curriculum as a chance for our students to acquire a range of capital – social, personal, emotional, cultural – then we are approaching it in the best way.

It is interesting to note that the root of the word 'curriculum' is the Latin verb *currere*, meaning 'to run'. As a noun, it meant 'racecourse', providing an indication of something that has a clear start and end point with challenge along the way. By the mid-nineteenth century, the word 'curriculum' was in regular use in European universities to describe not only the total programme of study undertaken or offered, but also the individual aspects therein; we all design an aspect of curriculum when we plan a lesson or a learning sequence.

However you choose to define or determine curriculum, you are doing so in abstract form: your definition may differ slightly from that of your colleagues, but there are still numerous concrete principles that need to be considered as you plan. Essentially, your curriculum encapsulates everything you offer that is an opportunity for pupils to learn something new. Through direct experience, instruction or practice, the curriculum can be argued to be as much about the inspiration and drive it offers teachers as the instruction and knowledge it imparts to those who study it.

So what?

An understanding of the history of curriculum development is far from essential for early career teachers (ECTs) – or indeed teachers of any experience – but it is useful to track the establishment of concepts, terms and approaches. Following is a very brief history.

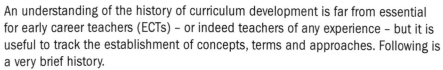

A history of curriculum

Plato

Although Plato's work predates the use of the word 'curriculum', it can be argued that with *The Republic*, Plato (428–348BC) produced the first coherent treatise on education in Western civilisation. Plato treats education as an integral, vital part of a wider picture of the well-being of society. Plato (2007) saw education's ultimate idea as the promotion of knowing the idea of good – that is, virtuousness. Plato posits a theory of what education means for both the individual and the state, focusing on the important role of those who must carefully choose the material to teach the future guardians of nations. Implicit in his philosophy of education is an underlying understanding of who is to be educated – a common theme even now, many centuries later. Plato makes it clear that the chosen material forms the 'curriculum', which is based on the recipient, not the donor. Plato advocates a more vocational programme of study, developing what he sees as the core skills essential to human function in society. However, despite not explicitly referring to it as a 'curriculum', Plato still advocates the order in which material should be taught – training the spirit and the body first, then introducing the more complex academic elements when the student has developed competency. He combines subjects and their introduction with the age and experience levels at which he wishes students to be exposed to them.

Reflective task ◄◄◄

- How do you view Plato's ideals through the lens of modern teaching and your own initial ideas as a teacher?

Furlong and Maynard (1995) espouse the view that the pre-service teacher goes through five developmental stages, the first of which is 'Early Idealism' – your idealistic desires to identify closely with pupils and their interests, perhaps emulating your own positive experiences as a pupil yourself, and those teachers and learning experiences that you most enjoyed.

As suggested above, an intimate knowledge of curriculum development is far from essential, but it is important. The pace of change in approaches and design, and the rhythms and direction of that change, should be noted. There is a strong and undeviating relationship between the curriculum of the past and the curriculum of today: the past, in curriculum-making, is far from a 'foreign country' where things are done differently.

Dewey

Let us now leap forward a few thousand years to the start of the twentieth century.

For John Dewey (1859–1952), democracy was a societal ideal, prevailing only when it enabled diverse groups to form common interests. It could be argued, perhaps, that a curriculum represents the agreed, intended, shared interests desired. In *Democracy and Education*, Dewey (1916) indicated that society needed schools for far more than the superficial reason of education. A highly influential figure in the progressive movement, Dewey's ideas were built around the learner being allowed to explore issues of their own desire or interest. However, it must be emphasised that Dewey's curriculum was far more than discovery learning: experiences had to be democratic and humane; they had to enhance growth, arouse curiosity and enable learners to create their own meanings. There are many elements of Dewey's work that now find themselves under the banner of cognitivism and thought. Dewey believed that 'thinking' was a skill to be taught, not just an instruction to be followed innately. Dewey developed these ideas into a model he referred to as the 'flexible curriculum' – the contextual features and purpose of education should be determined by the learners, not by the teachers. The following are the principal features of Dewey's model.

» Curriculum is based on the pupils' perceptions of their own interests.

» Curriculum enables pupils to engage fully in its design.

» Curriculum should be focused on practical activity and tasks that the pupil finds relevant.

» Curriculum should emphasise the importance of learning from a perspective of mindset – facing down difficulties, resolving problems.

» Curriculum should focus more on discovery and less on rote-learning.

Ultimately, Dewey felt the curriculum would have more meaning for those exposed to it if there were relevance and engagement in its design.

Tyler

Ralph Tyler's (1902–94) proposed model of curriculum development was simple and systematic. He advocated stripping design back to a well-ordered, structured approach that he referred to as the rational objective model (Tyler, 1949). Although seen by some as too mechanistic and focused on 'measures', Tyler sought to provide clarity at the heart of instruction. Central to Tyler's thinking was the idea that behavioural objectives should be formed that made the required learning outcomes very clear and unambiguous. This simplicity therefore made measurement and evaluation far easier. It could be depicted as shown in Figure 2.1.

Figure 2.1 Tyler's rational objective model

» *Objectives:* What is the purpose of the instruction?

» *Content:* What experiences, tasks or activities will attain this purpose?

» *Pedagogy:* How will these be organised and delivered to ensure effectiveness?

» *Assessment:* How can assessment be used to determine when the purposes are met?

In essence, Tyler's model requires the teacher to formulate objectives, select the content based on this, select the appropriate pedagogies based on the content, deliver instruction and then measure the outcomes. Simple.

Bruner

Jerome Bruner (1915–2016) is a seminal thinker and theorist who is most often associated with the concept of 'discovery learning'. Bruner (1960) extended his ideas into curriculum design with the spiral curriculum model. The essence of this model is that any subject can be taught effectively in some form to pupils at any stage of their development. The spiral model is simple in terms of description (although not necessarily so in implementation): information within a curriculum is structured in such a way as to introduce complex ideas at an initial simplified level, then revisit those ideas with increasing complexity as pupils build their knowledge and experience. Bruner suggested that each time a pupil revisits a topic, the information is reinforced and connections strengthened; there is a logical progression from simple to complex, so pupils are encouraged to apply foundational knowledge to later elements of the curriculum content. By focusing pupils' attention on the relevant elements of the content and then focusing on the resolution of problems, the intensity of learning can be increased.

In the view of the author, a spiral approach allows for pupil progression towards a predetermined set of standards or statements, laying the initial groundwork and conceptual terminology before revisiting the subject matter at regular intervals with increased practical application knowledge – a little like training to teach.

Taba

Hilda Taba (1902–67) is highly regarded. We explore more of her influence in subsequent chapters, but Taba's work is often known as the 'grassroots' model (Taba, 1962) because it places great store in the development of curriculum by teachers themselves – the pedagogues creating the bigger pictures. In doing so, they become more responsive and reactive to changes in context and student needs. Taba's model is based on a cycle of key elements (see below), and the emphasis is very much on continual, formative assessment of student progress along the intended curriculum, ensuring that all interactive elements of the cycle are compatible with the identified needs of the student. Taba's work was criticised for being too reliant on the infallibility of instruction from teachers, but many see her model as the genesis of concepts we would now group under the banner of 'responsive teaching'.

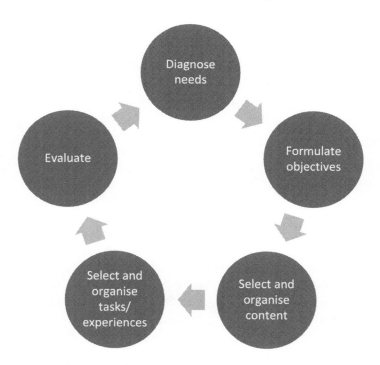

Figure 2.2 Taba's 'grassroots' cycle

Jackson

Philip Jackson (1928–2015) coined the term '*hidden curriculum*' (Jackson, 1968) to describe elements that were not obvious or visible to the pupil; he felt that some pupils would be reluctant to accept certain aspects as part of the learning process – namely rules, routines and regulations – and therefore these should be hidden from them as a valid method of developing autonomy. Naturally, critics abound – especially around the issue of transparency.

Jackson used principles such as the idea that some knowledge is beyond the capabilities of some pupils and that recall is the highest form of intellectual achievement. He also posited that authority holds sway and must be trusted, and that passive acceptance is a more desirable response than active criticism; moreover, he believed creativity and individual judgement are inconsequential and emotions are irrelevant.

Views of the controversial '*hidden curriculum*' can be softened somewhat if you acknowledge that there are some parts of any curriculum that *need* to happen but are not part of the planned curriculum as written – an acceptance, perhaps, that behaviour is a necessary companion to progress.

Reflective task ◀◀◀

Of the models outlined above, there will naturally be some that appeal and some that are anathema to your own core values and professional identity. However, as with any learning theory or approach, it is not a case of 'one size fits all' – or, indeed, nailing your colours to the mast of any specific ideology at the expense of all others. Being a teacher is an ever-developing and active process of enquiry, based on the simple premise that you should not only know *what* you are doing, but *why* you are doing it. Complete fidelity to one course of prescribed action smacks of compliance, which is a most dangerous and unsound defence for any decision in education.

- With that in mind, what aspects of the above models do you consider align with your thinking on curriculum development, and which go against it?

- Make a list of positive and negative elements and effects of each of the seminal models.

- What middle ground might you adopt?

Now what? ◀◀◀

Why is curriculum important to me as an early career teacher?

Put simply, curriculum is the concept; your pedagogy is the concrete. The very nature of curriculum is responsiveness, which is in the hands of the individual teacher. Curriculum is the broad field of concepts, but not necessarily the most efficient route to connect them all – that's the responsibility of the pedagogue.

The models we have explored so far in this chapter can be grouped into either 'product', where the outcomes are tangible and quantifiable, or 'process', where the main outcome is learner development. Whichever ideology you favour, never underestimate your role in the creation, delivery and evaluation of curriculum within your setting.

Curriculum is a complex concept, so it is important to be aware of how decisions are arrived at and the rationale behind the choices made; the shape and structure of the curriculum model has a direct influence on the structure of the content and the accompanying pedagogy and assessment that implements and validates it, all of which starts with the classroom teacher – you. The extent of your involvement in the initial planning and post-delivery evaluation processes will vary depending on the organisation and institution in which you work, but you must nevertheless place great store on being an informed practitioner, able to make decisions, articulate purposes and create positive curriculum experiences for pupils.

Practical task for tomorrow ◀◀◀

Look at your existing teaching plan for a forthcoming sequence, or reflect on a sequence you have recently taught.

- Was it designed with product or process as the outcome intention?

- How do you know?

- How effectively did your instruction enable it to meet those aims?

Practical task for next week ◀◀◀

Take Taba's (1962) cycle from earlier in this chapter. For each section, write down examples from your current teaching or from a recently taught topic.

- What needs were diagnosed?

- What objectives were formulated as a result of those diagnosed needs?

- What content was selected and how was it organised? What was the rationale for sequence of material through the topic?

- What tasks and activities were chosen to support the learning of the chosen content and the progress towards the intended objectives? Were the tasks fit for purpose?

- What evaluation was done after the teaching? What form did the evaluation take and how reliable was it as a measure of the effectiveness of the teaching? Did all pupils successfully access the curriculum?

Practical task for the longer term ◀◀◀

Focus on these prompts over the course of the next term. Consider what happens in your department/key stage as well as in your own classroom, and build your practice through focused reflection.

- What was the purpose of the designed curriculum in terms of skills and knowledge to be developed?

- How was the order in which material was taught determined? Who was involved in this process?

- How were the tasks that enabled demonstration of pupil learning of the content designed? How much autonomy for pedagogy did you have as an individual teacher of that element?

- Against what terms and outcomes was successful delivery of the curriculum measured?

What next? ◀ ◀ ◀

Further reading

Curriculum is a vast topic with many approaches and there have been a vast number of theorists and historians interested in the development of curriculum through the years.

A good starting point can be the works of those thinkers and practitioners whose work you have looked at in this chapter: Plato, Dewey, Bruner, Taba and Jackson.

Robinson, M (2013) *Trivium 21C: Preparing Young People for the Future with Lessons from the Past*. Carmarthen: Crown House. Robinson's work provides both philosophical and practical frameworks for curriculum design, drawing on the classic arts of grammar, dialectic and rhetoric.

References

Ausubel, D (1968) *Educational Psychology: A Cognitive View*. New York: Holt, Rinehart and Winston.

Bruner, J (1960) *The Process of Education*. Cambridge, MA: Harvard University Press.

Dewey, J (1916) *Democracy and Education*. New York: Macmillan.

Furlong, J and Maynard, T (1995) *Mentoring Student Teachers: The Growth of Professional Knowledge*. London: Routledge.

Jackson, P W (1968) *The Hidden Curriculum*. New York: Alfred A Knopf.

Plato (2007) *The Republic*. Harmondsworth: Penguin.

Taba, H (1962) *Curriculum Development: Theory and Practice*. New York: Harcourt, Brace & World.

Tyler, R W (1949) *Basic Principles of Curriculum and Instruction*. Chicago: University of Chicago Press.

Chapter 3   Behind the terms

Introduction

Whether you want to 'expose' your pupils to the curriculum, or simply give them 'access', a wealth of terminology accompanies design. Although curricula are enacted in classrooms, they exist on paper, so it is important that as a teacher, you have an understanding of the key terms, concepts and associated implications.

What? (The big idea)

Shared language and terminology

So let's dive further into the language itself. As mentioned above, you must look to avoid lethal mutations where concepts are dealt with or implemented with only surface-level understanding – those who use them without understanding them dilute them or destroy them. Training must support that necessary fundamental understanding, not just of the term but of the principles on which it is built; there are no new ideas in education, but not everybody knows the old ideas.

It is important to maintain both internal and external curriculum coherence – the internal coherence of the relationships and connections between the taught content and the external coherence of the relationships between the taught curriculum and its many and varied implementers and enactors. Curriculum goals direct practice, which leads to observed performance – evaluated against those goals – which in turn allows for targeted feedback – shaped by the goals – which then guides further practice in a cycle of improvement. The curriculum becomes the lead weight to which are tethered the various helium balloons that represent stakeholders in pupil development; without being secured to the curriculum through the string of shared language and understanding, they will float away.

In her excellent 'Professional Schools for Teachers' paper, Kennedy (1992, p 73), states that '*content provides the stuff of deliberation; the frames of reference for interpreting situations, the value judgments for selecting goals, and the principles for choosing among competing actions*'.

She goes on to remind us that '*even a decision to reject a particular principle or concept requires awareness of the principle and how it could be applied to a situation*'; we are confident in rejecting or dismissing ideas only when we truly understand them. She summarises by telling us that '*content provides the language for describing and interpreting experiences. If each teacher were left to deliberate in private, conversations among teachers would resemble a Tower of Babel.'*

So what? ◀◀◀

What are the key terms we need to understand when making curriculum choices?

Curriculum itself is a vast concept in its own right – it is difficult to sum it up accurately in a few lines but, as Einstein once said, if you can't explain something simply then you don't know it well enough.

Curriculum is only ever a model, a framework – it is not sacrosanct and it is never a finished article. It is defined by Ofsted (2019) as

> *the substance of what is taught. It is the specific plan of what learners need to know and should be able to do. The curriculum shapes and determines what learners of all ages will get out of their educational experience.*

A curriculum can simply be seen as a plan for learning, but it has numerous constituent parts and, depending on your world-view and educational perspective, many responsibilities – for example, the broadening of cultural capital. In its broadest sense, it defines and represents everything valued by the institution and a summary of its commitment to society – it is an inventory, an overview, a plan, a totality, an agreement pertaining to the quality of education, across a range of subjects and disciplines, that a pupil will receive – or is entitled to. It is important to note curriculum must be systematic and intentional. Curriculum is not some happy accident or a smorgasbord of concepts and ideas grabbed from a range of shelves and bundled together – at its heart are commitment, vision and dedication.

Let's outline some of the key concepts and terminology so you are confident when you discuss and reflect on curriculum decision-making.

First, let's consider the difference between *breadth* and *depth*. Breadth is the range of subjects taught across the entire curriculum and the span of knowledge within each subject. A broad curriculum therefore focuses on all curriculum subjects, not just core subjects. Breadth can also be seen within subjects, such as a global history curriculum covering a wide range of times and places, or English curriculum that covers a large range of authors and cultures. Depth, as it suggests, is how deeply specific topics within each subject are covered and studied – how well pupils understand key concepts, underlying links and so on. Depth is related to the intricacy and complexity of the schema formed during study to enable conceptual grasp and understanding.

Knowledge can be *substantive* (declarative) or *disciplinary* (procedural) – knowing 'what' and knowing 'how'. Substantive knowledge is content taught as fact – properties of materials, plots of plays, mathematical formulae; disciplinary knowledge is the understanding of how knowledge itself is established and verified – persuasive writing, conducting experiments.

Core knowledge comprises the basic facts to be learned and retained, while *hinterland knowledge* is contextual knowledge needed to provide deeper meaning, frame ideas and concepts, and give greater depth. For example, in a mathematics lesson, a pupil needs the core knowledge of displacement and volume theory to properly acquire and retain hinterland knowledge of the story of Archimedes.

Threshold concepts are similar to core knowledge in that they represent the entrance-level ideas – concepts that enable pupils to better understand other ideas; they need to know about 2D shapes before tackling 3D shapes.

Curriculum structures are important to understand as well. A vertical structure introduces curriculum aspects progressively as the school year develops, with knowledge built on prior learning. What pupils learn in lesson one is built on in lesson two – pupils learn about Elizabethan England before they tackle a Shakespeare play. A horizontal structure is more thematic, with aspects of curriculum introduced to pupils across year groups at the same time – perhaps a personal, social and health education (PSHE) theme or topic – to integrate and interrelate knowledge.

The curriculum can also be *cumulative* – knowledge builds on and expands previous learning; *segmented* – new ideas are added that are related to current contexts (so something a pupil learns on a geography field trip, or a one-off charity day leads to fundraising skills being developed); or *spiral* – previous learning is revisited and new knowledge added at age- or stage-appropriate times, such as persuasive writing being taught every year but with increasing complexity each time. If the curriculum is taught through the experiences and lives of the pupils, it is *context dependent*, and if it isn't related to personal experience, it is *context independent*.

Coherence is vitally important – it involves alignment and mutual reinforcement of all the moving parts. Coherence is an agreed aspect of high-functioning teams and schemes. It is also important to recognise the types of coherence – internal and external, as outlined above. For example, lesson observation needs an understanding of curriculum sequencing to provide an informed view of pupil development; different subject areas use different pedagogies to deliver the same set of curriculum aims.

It must be noted that the *specification* for a subject with an eye on summative assessment is not a curriculum – it is too passive; curriculum is active.

Specification is simply a list of required ingredients; the recipe is then followed (or adapted) in the respective external environments.

Reflective task ◄◄◄

Reflection is only possible when there is an agreed and shared framework through which to reflect – a language lens, perhaps.

- List any terms related to curriculum development that you have heard or been exposed to but don't truly understand.

- What effect does this have on you as a practitioner, and particularly on your self-efficacy?

- Make a list of terms that you are unsure of and set yourself the challenge of finding out what they mean to you.

Now what?

What are the implications of all this curriculum terminology and conceptual understanding for classroom practitioners? Teachers play an integral role in the development of curriculum and therefore the policy that governs it – statements of intent only go so far, and unless they are implemented in practice they are almost meaningless; this requires an active and very responsive process where teachers work from the initial principles, concepts and language and then develop and improve. Without an understanding of the fundamentals, teachers cannot construct the accurate mental models of expertise that are required to underpin their developing practice.

The curriculum thus rises above the definitions and the concept of being simply a 'product' that is uncritically and compliantly delivered by teachers to be something more real, more embodied – something that is in fact the result of decisions practitioners make in their classrooms. It is more of an impact than an intent.

Consider the word 'curriculum' as an optional prefix to – or focus for – other processes such as evaluation, monitoring, enquiry, development, alignment and scrutiny, but also as a living organism that grows and flourishes (or dies) in its environments. That is why, as cultivators of the environment, you need to know about curriculum. You need to know the terms, understand them and use them with confidence.

Many a question is begged every time curriculum is placed under the spotlight: What should schools be teaching? Why? What role does each subject, topic or domain play in the wider picture? Your role is to believe in the power of your subject(s) and convey that belief to your students.

Indeed, does curriculum have to be solely the result of the planned approach and predetermined content, or is it perhaps more than that? Is there room for responsiveness, spontaneity – even luck? If we agree that the curriculum is a total immersive experience, then I would argue that what happens under the banner of the classroom is part of the curriculum for the child. And, seeing that as much of what happens in the classroom is determined by, guided by, influenced by or affected by the teacher, you carry a significant weight of responsibility.

Knowledge or skills?

We hear much talk of a knowledge-rich curriculum, but what does this actually mean in theory and practice?

In 2021, Nick Gibb delivered a speech that explored the thinking and rationale behind the need for a '*knowledge-rich curriculum*', informed by the work of Ed Hirsch: '*It is our moral duty to teach [pupils] important facts and truths, delivered through a well-sequenced, knowledge-rich curriculum*' (Gibb, 2021). So, what defines 'knowledge-rich'? And where do skills lie in this? First, you cannot divorce skill from content; there is no specific part of our brain that does 'analysis' or 'evaluation'; it has to be underpinned by swathes of domain-specific understanding and, in essence, facts. Knowledge can be both declarative and/or procedural: declarative knowledge points to 'knowing what' (factual knowledge), while procedural knowledge to 'knowing how' (knowledge of specific functions and procedures to perform a complex process, activity or task).

A curriculum that is *knowledge rich* centres around pupils being able to acquire *powerful knowledge* (Young and Muller, 2013) across a range of subject areas and disciplines, therefore accessing a broad and balanced educational offer with concepts and ideas revisited with increasing complexity to deepen knowledge and understanding. As indicated above, knowledge has to be taught in domains alongside the requisite skills to ensure there is more focus on long-term learning and less on performance; it has been argued that in the past there has been too much emphasis on skill without the necessary foundational knowledge to develop mastery. Therefore, each subject area has its own curriculum, in which the knowledge is used to help develop the skill – for example, the process of evaluation in GCSE English literature is very specific to English literature, and the elements are not immediately transferable to, say, GCSE statistics or BTEC design and technology. Indeed, we are exposing pupils to what we deem necessary to love a subject; the capacity or ability to understand the material in a text does not stand separately from the text itself, but rather accompanies the text – the understanding differs from text to text, as the content within them is not the same. Therefore, skill comes from knowledge, not the other way around.

As the knowledge-rich curriculum calls for pupils attaining a broad understanding of the more 'traditional' academic subjects over the course of their study, it is essential that the knowledge is subject based; every discipline and domain has its own content, with pupils learning specialised concepts within each subject area across the arts, languages, humanities and sciences. In line with the agreed principles of cognitive science that underpin much of the Early Career Framework (ECF) and Initial Teacher Education (ITE), the knowledge-rich curriculum is logically and carefully constructed to build new knowledge on existing knowledge, increasing the complexity and therefore the depth of processing and strength of schema. This is where curriculum and pedagogy begin to become more significantly intertwined, as the approach taken by the teacher to support the cognitive process is essential – in essence, how can teachers ensure that knowledge taught in their classrooms will be remembered successfully and accurately in the years to come?

This is why the Key Stage 1 teacher works hard drilling pupils on their times tables, as the Year 8 mathematics teacher needs to be sure that these are readily available in order to work on aspects of algebra; the Year 4 teacher starts to look at cell structure and the Year 9 biology teacher increases the complexity.

A knowledge-rich curriculum is centred around the academic; it must be taught by teachers who have sufficient expertise in their discipline, but also possess what Shulman (1986) calls the 'pedagogical content knowledge' (PCK) that is unique to the pedagogue – they know not only what to teach but how best to transmit this to their students and check for the evidence of learning. Teachers are always learning, as pupils are never the same from year to year – what worked pedagogically for one set of Year 6 children may not work for another; the GCSE specification may not change in terms of content, but the manner of delivery – the pedagogy – will alter responsively according to the academic need or ability of those in the group. In recent times, the focus on a knowledge-rich curriculum has led to a more teacher-led approach in classrooms, leaving behind concepts such as 'discovery learning' in favour of more direct (with a small 'd') instructional methods.

In essence, curriculum doesn't happen by accident; it is active and carefully considered – it is deliberate.

Practical task for tomorrow ◀◀◀

Skill cannot and should not be divorced from content; skills are not necessarily transferable, but instead draw on the content taught. Therefore, words take on new meanings – to evaluate a text in English is not the same as to evaluate an experiment in science or evaluating the success of fieldwork in geography. These are called 'command words' – words that give a student an instruction to *do* something. Students are entitled, within their learning, to know what these key terms mean in order to attain that important cultural and curricula literacy necessary to access content.

- What are the command words in your subject?

- How do you teach them and their meanings to students?

- Make a table like the one below to help you reflect and develop.

Word	Meaning	Example	How I teach it	What I could do better
Evaluate	Make a judgement; weigh up the evidence	'Evaluate' the text to decide the extent to which you agree with the statement	Ideas of making judgements and using evidence, then examples of completed evaluations	Make it more explicit; focus on the skill alongside the knowledge of a text, not just in isolation

Practical task for next week ◀◀◀

When Young and Muller (2013) referenced 'powerful knowledge', they did not mean knowledge of the powerful – rather that this powerful knowledge comes from experience, growth and centuries of learning by others, therefore being independent of changing contexts and times. What is the 'powerful knowledge' in your domain for each year group? How can this be developed in students?

Using a specification for your subject, consider the following prompts.

- How does each element of the content provide a foundation for future learning and development?

- Why is this content deemed 'powerful knowledge'?

- How is this content significantly superior to the basic knowledge necessary for everyday life? Why are students 'better' for knowing this?

- How well do you understand the content you are teaching your pupils?

Practical task for the longer term ◄◄◄

The final question in the previous task is essential for your consideration as an early career teacher (ECT), and then throughout the rest of your career. How well do you understand the content you are teaching? You cannot possibly know absolutely everything there is to know about what you teach, so you are professionally obliged to be active and 'in touch' with developments in your domains.

Identify priority areas of your curriculum where you feel your knowledge may be challenged or found wanting; complete a SWOT (below) and consider how and where you will seek support to develop your weaknesses and offset your threats, as in the example below.

Subject area: geography – Year 5	
Strengths	**Weaknesses**
Terminology – locational knowledge and places Fieldwork	Human geography – not strong on settlement and land use or economic aspects
Opportunities	**Threats**
Can develop technical terms in Year 5s Creation of quizzes and vocabulary tests	Teaching the Trade Links lessons in Week 5

What next? ◄ ◄ ◄

Further reading

Simons, J and Porter, N (eds) (2015) *Knowledge and the Curriculum: A Collection of Essays to Accompany E D Hirsch's Lecture at Policy Exchange*. London: Policy Exchange. [online] Available at: https://policyexchange.org.uk/wp-content/uploads/2016/09/knowledge-and-the-curriculum.pdf (accessed 15 February 2023).

References

Gibb, N (2021) The Importance of a Knowledge-Rich Curriculum. [online] Available at: www.gov.uk/government/speeches/the-importance-of-a-knowledge-rich-curriculum (accessed 18 January 2023).

Kennedy, M M (1992) Establishing Professional Schools for Teachers. In Levine, M (ed), *Professional Practice Schools* (pp 63–80). New York: Teachers College Press.

Ofsted (2019) Education Inspection Framework 2019: Inspecting the Substance of Education. [online] Available at: www.gov.uk/government/consultations/education-inspection-framework-2019-inspecting-the-substance-of-education/education-inspection-framework-2019-inspecting-the-substance-of-education (accessed 15 February 2022).

Shulman, L (1986) Those Who Understand: Knowledge Growth in Teaching. *Educational Researcher*, 15(2): 4–14.

Young, M and Muller, J (2013) On the Powers of Powerful Knowledge. *Review of Education*, 1(3): 229–50.

Chapter 4   Principles of curriculum design

Introduction

Once a curriculum has been contemplated, it must be designed. You must consider the purpose of curriculum and the foundations on which you will build your models, whether broad across a subject or focused within an aspect or topic from that domain. This may mean you take the existing model and examine it closely, with a need to assimilate new content into it or allow the existing model to accommodate new ideas. It might mean ripping it up and starting again. Whatever your approach to design, it must be started with a clear idea of the ultimate purpose of the curriculum and how it will respond to the needs of pupils, help them progress and develop them as individuals.

For example, Paulo Freire (1970) suggested that curriculum planning was a fully people-oriented process in which the starting point was the students, and their expectations and wants. He believed that curriculum planning was an ongoing process that could be done through mutual participation of teachers and pupils. How practical is this?

What? (The big idea)

A close examination of curriculum planning over the past decades would show a very clear but quite slow and deliberate move from the 'drifting' practices of previous generations to an approach with far more consideration and action – the need for curriculum to not only deliver the necessary knowledge but also reflect the changing societal times. There is perhaps more structured evolution, as opposed to knee-jerk revolutions every now and then.

In order to plan your curriculum, you must engage with the big ideas that underpin your classroom practice; if you, as the teacher, are the first point of pupils' contact with a curriculum, then you must know the principles upon which your pedagogy is built. It is not enough to know what; you also need to know why. Compliance is an unsound defence that stems from merely doing as you are told without consideration of your context or your intended outcomes. Curriculum delivery may come with challenges to your existing beliefs and practices – to face a challenge, you must understand where came from and why it is a challenge. In order to help you consider where your practice falls within the wider scope of the curriculum, it may be useful to consider the spider's web, as proposed by Thijs and van den Akker (2009) (see Figure 4.1).

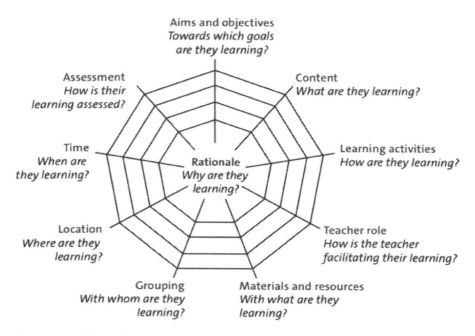

Figure 4.1 Thijs and van den Akker's (2009) curricular spider's web

The model is helpful, as it shows us the full range of practices and implications that you must consider as you forge your curriculum. It is also helpful to consider the practice of curriculum-making as a design process with a tangible outcome, not just an exercise in paperwork; it is active and alive, it responds and breathes, it is wrought not written. A road map poster on a classroom wall is all very well, but it is no indication of curriculum effectiveness in terms of transmission or reception.

A further useful philosophy to consider in terms of the principles by which curriculum is designed is Occam's razor: the simplest answer is often the best. Too often, there are needless complexities and levels of process behind educational decision-making – we are far better to operate by a principle of less is more, with a lean, sharp approach – what are the smallest number of steps pupils need to take to reach the next milestone? By reducing the noise of the curriculum and instead amplifying the signal of its component parts, we remove the need for excessive instructions and focus more on what can be seen as better structures and frameworks. A classroom task is at its best when it allows the student to simply exemplify what it is they have learnt, in line with what you intended to teach them.

Engelmann and Carnine (1991, p vi) tell us:

> Teaching is the process that follows the specifications provided by the curriculum. The relationship is simple: the teaching must transmit to the students all the new skills and knowledge specified in the curriculum.

A test of a valid curriculum would show that students did not have specific knowledge and skills before the teacher taught them. The post-test that is presented after instruction shows that students uniformly have the skills.

The conclusion is that a process occurred between the pre-test and post-test and caused the specific changes in student performance.

So what?

Teaching is the mouthpiece of the conceived curriculum; in order to successfully walk the walk, you must also talk the talk – you must know what you are referring to but also the thinking behind it and the implications enmeshed within it. As an early career teacher (ECT), it is worth being familiar with the curriculum elements within the Early Career Framework (ECF), particularly regarding your specific subject or phase; this will allow you to then make informed and pertinent choices related to curriculum design – for example, 'how' pupils will acquire and demonstrate the new knowledge.

A knowing of 'why' as well as 'what' increases your agency as a teacher – the classroom is indeed a layer of the curriculum, and as a teacher you can be collaborative in the process of curriculum design. It is the teacher who demonstrates to the pupils the meaningful connections between the knowledge and the skills in your area, or the way the new learning of the day builds on what has gone before.

The principles of curriculum design, therefore, must pay heed to the varying areas in which the intent will be realised and the respective evidence bases on which the intent and implementation are built. Only then can the design give the best chance of the impact being as desired. Consider the image of an iceberg: the classroom environment and those within it are the tip, but there is a great deal hidden below the surface. That includes the evidence that underpins the decisions made about how progress is defined; or where the challenge lies; or how the content can and might need to be differentiated; or how the chosen sequence is best for the development of knowledge; or how the knowledge and skills complement and develop each other.

Within design comes the need for that progression – hence the concept of the road map favoured by so many as a visual – and how that progression can promote the development of the schema: the reiteration, integration and deepening of core concepts. Curriculum is more granular than simply the 'road map'. There is no explicit reference to curriculum sequencing within the ECF evidence base – when the sequence is referred to, it is perhaps less focused around the 'correct order in which to do things' (which has never been scientifically justified) and more around the development of thought, building knowledge upon prior knowledge underpinned by experience. To one person, there may be a logical sequence of components within topics or concepts, but one person's logic is another's muddle. This is why curriculum is important: it is the enabler of individual pedagogues, unique practitioners. Curriculum must be flexible, adaptable, exportable – what exists on the page of intent never survives completely intact in the action of implementation.

Much of curriculum is thus developed from what you believe about the purposes of education, because if pedagogy is curriculum, your pedagogy is fuelled by your core beliefs. Korthagen (2004) refers to an 'onion' model of competencies (see Figure 4.2).

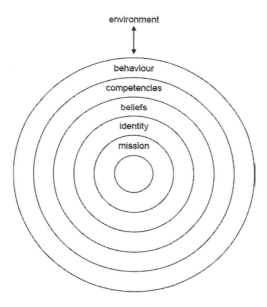

Figure 4.2 Korthagen's 'onion' model of competencies

From this we can see that, working both ways, our behaviour and our competencies influence and are influenced by our core 'mission' as a teacher, and from that our identity and what we believe – 'consciously we teach what we know, subconsciously we teach who we are' (Hamachek, 1999, p 209).

As you start to design your curriculum, you will start to consider what knowledge is most worthwhile, from that what counts as knowledge – what is essential and what can simply be alluded to or signalled. Remember, too, that we consider skills as types of knowledge – ways of enacting or demonstrating knowledge. From this you may then question the purpose of education in your eyes – after all, you have chosen to enter the profession for a reason.

When you know what you believe, you will consciously sculpt your curriculum according to your priorities. Remember that the goal of curriculum is enabling pupils to learn its content. Given that this learning is a slow and largely invisible process, you will need to monitor pupils continually as they move through the curriculum – it is a cumulative process. Therefore, each stage of the curriculum must be built on and reinforce what went before in the simplest and most straightforward way possible.

Reflective task ◀◀◀

Think back to the spider's web metaphor (Figure 4.1).

- Use it as a framework for reflecting on a recently taught concept or element from your course.

- Can you answer each of the questions posed with a degree of certainty and satisfaction?

Now what? ◀◀◀

In his work on principled curriculum design, Dylan Wiliam (2013) proposes the following seven 'principles', operating in tension with each other. The curriculum is:

1. *balanced* – it promotes all development as equal; intellectual, moral, spiritual, aesthetic, creative, emotional, physical;

2. *rigorous* – subject matter is taught in a way faithful to its discipline;

3. *coherent* – explicit connections are made between the different subjects and experiences;

4. *vertically integrated* – progression is secured through clarity and carefully sequenced knowledge;

5. *appropriate* – challenge is aligned to pupils' ability;

6. *focused* – big ideas and key concepts are identified and prioritised;

7. *relevant* – the intended outcomes are appropriate for those to whom it is being taught.

These are just examples, but they provide a strong basis for curriculum development. Posner and Rudnitsky (2001, p 8) argue that *'the curriculum indicates what is to be learned, the goals indicate why it is to be learned, and the instructional plan indicates how to facilitate learning'* and that a key component is that *'curriculum development entails selection and organization of a set of intended learning outcomes'*. In other words, know where you are going before you set off.

Marsh and Willis (2007) use the framework of a curriculum being a composite of three parts: planned, enacted and experienced. *Planned* refers to the intentions for the classroom, *enacted* to the actions within the classroom and *experienced* to how what happens in the classroom influences the individuals within it. Curriculum is complex, but it needn't be. As we know from Occam's razor, the simplest solution is often the best.

Going back to the spider's web, then, we have at the centre the 'rationale': why are pupils learning? This is the core principle: if there is no 'why', then there is definitely no purposeful 'what'. All other considerations stem from this one element – why. This, in turn, takes us back to those reflections on the necessary powerful knowledge for our subject or phase: what is the purpose of this as part of the chosen content? Teachers need to make sense of the chosen knowledge and also understand its reason for being there – why is it powerful for pupils to know about erosion? Why must pupils understand the concept of profit and loss? Why is the concept of worship so vital? What does it matter if pupils don't know the structure of a leaf?

These may be slightly futile questions as the very nature of the existence of specifications and a national curriculum for each subject take much of the determination of what should be taught out of the hands of individual teachers, but there is certainly still an element of flexibility or choice – although the aims of the curriculum from a summative perspective are nationally derived (even academies will not stray too far from the tree), they can be adopted and adapted by schools at an institutional level and then reshaped to meet the needs of different learners. This is why too much centralisation or genericism can be a bad thing; the truth is that one size fits very few.

One of the key areas of the spider's web is resources – what teachers and schools have to enable the curriculum to be taught; in essence, the resources shape the curriculum, given that it is dependent on them. Resources refer to a number of things, both internal and external. The best resource in any classroom, of course, is the teacher – when the smartboard breaks or the internet goes down, the teacher still has the internal store of requisite knowledge and the pedagogical content knowledge required to deliver the curriculum. Resources can be in the form of materials such as textbooks, technologies, scaffolds and tasks, and also in the form of the cognitive frameworks that currently exist in some form in the minds of the pupils – their prior knowledge, their experiences, their beliefs, their assumptions and their perceptions. It is essential that we, as teachers, have an understanding of the basic cognitive principles that are known to influence the development of knowledge in pupils: the need to pay attention to content that is to be learned, the need to accommodate it for a short time in working memory, grapple with it as one would materials in a workshop, then process and transfer it into long-term memory – the warehouse. In this warehouse, it may just sit and gather dust unless it is regularly retrieved and recalled, dusted off. All of this has implications for our principles of design: we have to accommodate these processes through the choices we make, enabling pupils to build concepts and mental models of expertise.

Beyond the material and cognitive resources are the relational resources – the public and semi-private worlds of the classroom (Nuthall, 2007) need to be recognised, accommodated, planned for. These include how students perceive the material and their relationship to it; how they perceive and interact in their environment and their relationship with it; and how students and teachers interact and perceive each other, and their formal and relational authorities.

Coe et al (2019) see curriculum as a planned concept. It looms large in their *Great Teaching Toolkit: Evidence Review.* Dimension 1, 'Understanding the Content' states that, as a teacher, you should have '*Knowledge of the requirements of curriculum sequencing and dependencies in relation to the content and ideas you are teaching*' (Coe et al, 2019, p 18), which '*involves knowing and being able to explain the dependencies and connections among different parts of the curriculum, and hence the requirements for sequencing*'. This knowledge is exemplified in '*curriculum planning, schemes of work and lesson plans that depend on correct sequencing and planned reactivation of prior knowledge*'. We can't just build our house on shifting sand: we need to be sure of our footing and take deliberate steps to construct experiences for pupils that enable them to attain – and retain – the knowledge we have elected to include.

You cannot and must not divorce the concept of planning a curriculum with clear principles from the daily lives of pupils. Nuthall (2007, p 35) reminds us that '*effective teaching means students learn what you intend them to learn*' and that '*learning, of whatever kind, is about change, and unless you know what has changed in the minds, skills and attitudes of your [pupils], you cannot really know how effective you have been*'.

All curriculum therefore comes down to what you intend as a teacher and how that intention manifests not only in your decisions, actions and attitudes in the classroom, but also in the way you measure the outcomes and the impact. Your view of success is determined by what you set out to achieve: all systems are perfectly designed to get the results they get. It is not enough to know what, you have to know why – compliance is an unsound defence.

Practical task for tomorrow ◀◀◀

You considered Korthagen's (2004) model of competencies, and in particular the 'core beliefs'. What are your core beliefs? What do you believe is the purpose of education? How much control over the impact of your own views do you have in terms of the way they manifest in your teaching?

Try to complete these sentences in simple terms.

- I believe the purpose of education to be ...

- I demonstrate this in my classroom by ...

Practical task for next week ◀◀◀

Every journey starts with a single step. Look ahead to your next set of teaching, your short-term curriculum. On what evidence and principles is this curriculum built? What are its aims?

Answer the following questions.

- To what extent have you determined the content of these lessons?

- If you haven't determined the content, who has?

- What evidence is being used to build the content of this curriculum?

- On what pedagogical principles are the lesson objectives based?

- What is the educational aim of this sequence within the curriculum? How will you know whether you have been successful in enabling all pupils to meet the intentions of the sequence?

Practical task for the longer term ◀◀◀

When you decided to enter the teaching profession and engage in Initial Teacher Education (ITE), you probably had a set of ready-formed ideals about the impact you would have, based largely on your own experience as a student. These ideals were largely formed out of the way you perceived your own teachers and the beliefs about education they were able to project onto you. If we subconsciously teach 'who we are', who are you? What were those early ideals and how true to them are you still?

- Try keeping a set of notes alongside your lesson plans, where you reflect closely on the way your core beliefs as a teacher were manifested in how you designed the experiences for the students, how you therefore enabled them access to the planned curriculum and how much of the curriculum was shaped by what you set in the way of tasks.

What next?

Further reading

Nuthall, G (2007) *The Hidden Lives of Learners*. Wellington: NZCER Press. Much of Nuthall's work is valid across a range of contexts, so it is highly recommended for any teacher. However, his ideas around the individual nature of learning make it a useful reference for setting out with curriculum.

References

Coe, R, Rauch, C, Kime, S and Singleton, D (2019) *Great Teaching Toolkit: Evidence Review.* Evidence Based Education. [online] Available at: https://assets.website-files.com/5ee28 729f7b4a5fa99bef2b3/5ee9f507021911ae35ac6c4d_EBE_GTT_EVIDENCE%20REV IEW_DIGITAL.pdf (accessed 14 February 2023).

Engelmann, S and Carnine, D (1991) *Theory of Instruction; Principles and Applications.* Eugene, OR: NIFDI Press.

Freire, P (1970) *Pedagogy of the Oppressed.* Harmondsworth: Penguin.

Hamachek, D (1999) Effective Teachers: What They Do, How They Do It, and the Importance of Self-knowledge. In Lipka, R P and Brinthaupt, T M (eds), *The Role of Self in Teacher Development* (pp 189-224). Albany, NY: State University of New York Press.

Korthagen, F (2004) In Search of the Essence of a Good Teacher: Towards a More Holistic Approach in Teacher Education. *Teaching and Teacher Education* 20: 77-97.

Marsh, C and Willis, G (2007) *Curriculum: Alternative Approaches, Ongoing Issues* (4th ed). Upper Saddle River, NJ: Pearson/Merrill Prentice Hall.

Nuthall, G (2007) *The Hidden Lives of Learners*. Wellington: NZCER Press.

Posner, G and Rudnitsky, A (2001) *Course Design: A Guide to Curriculum for Teachers.* New York: Longman.

Thijs, A and van den Akker, J (2009) *Curriculum in Development.* Enschede: SLO.

Wiliam, D (2013) *Principled Curriculum Design.* London: SSAT.

Chapter 5   Curriculum intent: setting out the goals

*The role of the teacher in 'curriculum-making' is to create a 'fruitful encounter'
between the content and the learner leading to a 'deeper understanding
of the world, modifications in perspectives and the cultivation of human
capacities or powers.*

(Deng, 2022, p 607)

*[Intent is] a framework for setting out the aims of a programme of education,
including the knowledge and understanding to be gained at each stage.*

(Ofsted, 2022a)

What? (The big idea)

No subject is the same, so one size of curriculum model fits very few. This is a
big problem. Principles are often able to be manifested in a range of different
domains, but we cannot move to the next stage with a basic framework within
which all subjects must be aligned – and this does each subject a disservice.
Some subjects are nicely hierarchical – take mathematics, for example, where
pupils need to know how to add and subtract before they can manipulate
fractions. Or units in geography, where pupils will only understand lake formation
if they first know the water cycle. Some subjects, however, do not behave in such
a hierarchical way. Take history, which is more cumulative – the concept of a
revolution can be taught at any point using Russia. Then, when the pupil is exposed
to France in the 1790s, they already have the relevant concepts within schema,
ready to be adapted for new domains. This sort of dichotomy is at the very heart
of teaching: the simplest answer (Occam's razor again) is that all new knowledge
has to be built on existing knowledge – it is your role as a teacher, as you design
and implement your curriculum, to be aware of that prior knowledge and act
accordingly. What students learn is a product of what they already know and what
you lay down to be taught – the intent.

What is intent?

What is 'intent'? The Early Career Framework (ECF) (Department for Education, 2019, p 12) states:

> *A school's curriculum enables it to set out its vision for the knowledge, skills and values that its pupils will learn, encompassing the national curriculum within a coherent wider vision for successful learning.*

Posner and Rudnitsky (2001, p 9) state that, '*Curriculum development results in a design specifying the desired learnings (the intended learning outcomes); thus, curriculum is analogous to a blueprint or an architectural design.*' Our ambitions of successfully realising the place of curriculum within the classroom are ultimately only as good as the plans we lay to stake that claim – we cannot just turn up in our teaching spaces and deliver what we wish, in the hope that – because we have determined that it is 'powerful knowledge' and therefore of value – it will be taken to heart by the pupils, that they will immediately see its value and commit it to their minds. No, we have to plan: planning makes the conceptual possible; it makes the vision a reality. Curriculum intent is just that – what we intend to teach, and what we intend that pupils will learn. We know that they will only learn their interpretation of what we teach, so we have to enter this process in the knowledge that individual learners will engage and understand in different ways; the curriculum will have to be adapted at the implementation phase, so we have to accommodate that in the way we design it. Again, Occam's razor applies: simple is better.

The most coherent curricula are designed with the idea of learning over time; each small curriculum in each subject area, key stage or domain merely sets the stage for what will come after. There are keys to all doors, but the right key opens the right door and no one has a master key for all educational doors; the curriculum is perhaps the locksmith – the individual charged with the opening of the right doors for the right people at the right time.

Below are some statements from Ofsted regarding curriculum intent.

> *Inspectors will make a judgement on the quality of education by evaluating the extent to which ...*

> - *leaders take on or construct a curriculum that is ambitious and designed to give all learners, particularly the most disadvantaged and those with special educational needs and/or disabilities (SEND) or high needs, the knowledge and cultural capital they need to succeed in life*

- *the provider's curriculum is coherently planned and sequenced towards cumulatively sufficient knowledge and skills for future learning and employment*

- *the provider has the same academic, technical or vocational ambitions for almost all learners. Where this is not practical – for example, for some learners with high levels of SEND – its curriculum is designed to be ambitious and to meet their needs*

- *learners study the full curriculum. Providers ensure this by teaching a full range of subjects for as long as possible, 'specialising' only when necessary.*
  (Ofsted, 2022a)

Ofsted intent statement

Inspectors will consider the knowledge and skills that pupils will gain at each stage through the school's curriculum (we call this 'intent'). They will look at the scope of the curriculum, including how carefully leaders have thought about what end points the curriculum is building towards (with reference to the national curriculum and, where relevant, the EYFS). They will also look at how leaders have broken down the content into components and sequenced that content in a logical progression, systematically and explicitly, for all pupils to acquire the intended knowledge and skills. Inspectors will also consider the rigour of subject-specific planning.

(Ofsted, 2022a)

So what? ◀ ◀ ◀

If the curriculum is the content, then the teaching of that curriculum becomes the transmission of the content; this has to be a clear signal that can be received by all. The curriculum is perhaps the model for progress that pupils will look to emulate and exceed, so we have to ensure that the statements of intent at every level are appropriate to the intended recipients – the delivery of the curriculum is not as generic as the intent may appear. The overall aim of the curriculum and its delivery should be the advancement of pupil learning through the most efficient and effective means. As a teacher, you are looking to motivate pupils to attend to the to-be-learned content, process it, grapple with it and transfer it to long-term memory, thereby supporting the creation of those complex and multi-connected mental models we refer to as schemata through our implementation.

Implementation and impact cannot manifest without intent, so you will need to recognise the thread that binds them; your intent statements mustn't be too hard to implement, but it is also important to understand the need for ambition within the intent, supported by effective implementation – nothing in education works in isolation.

Intent statements must be achievable, tangible versions of the specifications and/ or content requirements. If an intent statement is too diffuse or abstract, then it paves the way for poor implementation; clarity is the key to coherence, and ambiguity a recipe for anarchy. Intent is the planning stage – the vision for the teaching that will follow.

According to the Ofsted Handbook (Ofsted, 2022b), 'Good' intent has the following features:

» a curriculum that is ambitious for all pupils;

» a curriculum that is coherently planned and sequenced;

» a curriculum that is successfully adapted, designed and developed for pupils with special educational needs and/or disabilities;

» a curriculum that is broad and balanced for all pupils.

In essence, you can boil intent down to a simple question: What is my curriculum trying to achieve?

You need routines to 'quiet the tyranny of the urgent' (Hummel, 1994, p 1) in order to ensure that your intent can be implemented and have impact by ensuring you plot a path of highest challenge but least resistance, seeing every individual lesson plan as a microcosm of the wider curriculum goals.

At school level, there can be three starting points:

1. *a content curriculum* – specification of content to be taught as a starting point;

2. *an outcomes curriculum* – specification of outcomes to be achieved as a starting point;

3. *a process curriculum* – specification of long-term goals and educational purposes as a starting point; content and methods are then selected that are 'fit for purpose'.

(Stenhouse, 1975)

It is important for teachers to be aware of the fact that the curriculum is far more than just the content; it also encompasses the instructional methods, the learning activities and the assessment tools we will use to validate it – these are explored further across the next three chapters, which examine implementation. A curriculum exists because of its goals, so *'beliefs about what is needed to accomplish them should guide each step in curriculum planning and implementation'* (Brophy, 2000, p 14). We align our components with our intent, and we select them because we believe they are the best available means of helping pupils accomplish the overall goals within the intent.

These goals can have at their heart what could be seen as the *'transformative potential of education'* (Cuthbert and Standish, 2021, p 39): how the acquisition of concepts, language and models of thought changes the way pupils interpret and interact with their own world, and ones that they will go on to discover. Your role as a teacher is to understand first the context of your curriculum and then how this influences its intent – how well do you both understand and align with your school's mission for teaching?

Reflective task ◀ ◀ ◀

You can diagnose potential issues with your curriculum intent through posing and responding to some key questions:

- Describe the way the curriculum in your subject/phase has been designed. Why has it been designed using that model? For example, what considerations have been made for context, school vision, staff experience and expertise?

- Is the curriculum 'broad and balanced'? How do you know? Can you give an example?

- What do you want your pupils to know, understand and demonstrate by the time they finish the unit of work or topic? Take this broader – what should they know, understand and demonstrate in your subject by the time they leave the key stage?

- How is the curriculum sequenced in terms of planning for goals? Do you have a range of planning models – long, medium and short term? How much control over the manipulation of the intent statements do you have as an individual classroom teacher? Do you work from a term overview or a unit overview?

- How is your curriculum designed to develop both pupils' knowledge and their attitudes to learning, as well as their metacognitive abilities?

- How do you plan to ensure all pupils make progress? How do you diagnose their existing needs before planning your next steps?

Now what?

Supporting curriculum intent with available resources is vital. Plan for existing scenarios, not utopian ideals. Yes, you can adapt and change, but curriculum needs to happen – the intent must therefore be ambitious in scope but pragmatic in terms of practical aspects of implementation; you can intend to broaden the horizons of your pupils from the safety of the classroom, but you must also recognise and accommodate the principle of equity in terms of the pupils you teach. Every pupil is different, requiring different levels of support, socio-economic foundations and so on. At all times, your curriculum intent must be to include all pupils.

Diversity and cultural capital

A strong, broad and balanced curriculum will incorporate opportunities to enrich and nurture the cultural capital of students, as well as helping them meet their academic goals. Cultural capital can be defined as '*the essential knowledge that pupils need to be educated citizens, introducing them to the best that has been thought and said, and helping to engender an appreciation of human creativity and achievement*' (Ofsted, 2022b), which is a very ambitious scope indeed. However, you can see it as an opportunity to broaden the horizons and therefore connections available to the students you teach - you must develop a shared understanding of what cultural capital means across the school community, which in turn will help you to evaluate your approach and plan further opportunities to enhance it in your curriculum. For example, the GCSE English literature syllabus is very heavy on 'dead white men'; how can teachers go beyond the reaches of the specification and introduce diversity, a range of cultural voices that are more representative of the demographics you teach or – just as vitally – wider than the demographic you teach?

Culture is broad, so many opportunities are available to embed references and connections across the topics within your curriculum - it isn't just about trips to an art gallery or an understanding of Shakespeare. You must consider how you are preparing your pupils to live and thrive in culturally and ethnically diverse modern Britain. Any definition of 'culture' should be inclusive of, and relevant to, your whole school community. To avoid cultural capital becoming a 'bolt-on', you can use it as one of the sticks in your curriculum intent bundle. Work with it from the outset to ensure proper implementation through valid connections, within and across subjects, established in the intent. Curriculum intent must be planned carefully to develop the cultural capital of the pupils and in doing so allow them to access the material at more than simply surface level – it is almost a duty! By not providing or teaching the 'essential' knowledge and the 'standard reference points', we are locking pupils out of the learning process – just because it has a fancy name doesn't mean it is anything new; pupils need facts in order to solve problems and curriculum needs structure. If anything, it could be argued that the cultural capital becomes the spine from which the ribs of the curriculum spread – it holds it all together. However, it cannot simply be seen as an adjunct to tick a box; rather, the necessary 'knowledge' for pupils is driven hugely by the context of their learning and subject matter in each domain. You cannot teach 'cultural capital' lessons; instead, you need to ensure that you have factored in appropriate ways of determining the existing knowledge base of pupils and then – through instruction and providing opportunities for practice, coupled with relevant and effective feedback – embedded the cultural capital within the framework of the learning.

There is a lot of cultural inequality to deal with in daily practice. For example, I am an English teacher. When teaching the AQA GCSE poetry anthology to my group of culturally diverse Year 10s, I noticed that I was spending much of my time filling in gaps in knowledge before even scratching the surface of the meaning of the poems themselves. How can a 14 year-old pupil from a disadvantaged background analyse a poem by Seamus Heaney that makes subtle references to Irish political upheaval if they don't even know where Ireland is or how it is divided? The key rule, as ever, is never to assume. Novices build their schema from scratch, so too much too soon overloads the working memory and hinders learning. Identify the existing knowledge base, add to it, then develop – start by teaching the vocabulary and the concepts, then begin the analysis; start with the over-arching themes, then zoom into the details.

Teachers must take heed of this and plan knowledge provision in a suitable way, ensuring it is relevant for the context in which the learning is taking place – simply loading 'culture' on 'culture' with no thought to context or application will just overload pupils and negatively impact their learning experiences. Life is a rich tapestry, and it is your role to help them see how it is woven! Much of the acquisition of cultural capital is also social – learning is more than knowing what to do; it also involves knowing how to do it (Zimmerman, 1989) and this must also be considered. How can teachers and leaders use extra-curricular opportunities and pastoral work to enhance the pupil knowledge base? Zimmerman's piece concludes that pupils learn from observing others, so you have to make sure you are careful about what they observe! Clear modelling, guided practice and concrete examples are the bedrock of appropriate cultural capital instruction – novice learners need to see the building blocks, the stages, the constituent parts of each skill or concept; this comes from well-planned lessons and an appropriately structured curriculum.

The classroom must also monitor the acquisition of concepts and ideas from external social sources – it is well researched and shown that pupils bring their own perceptions and emotional responses to learning environments built on their prior experiences, which in turn can affect both their cognitive ability to process ideas and their ability to pay attention – you need to ensure that you plan relevant, stimulating and rich content that acknowledges the different domains of learning and knowledge acquisition. Providing cultural capital is more than just the role of the teacher: the pastoral team, the support staff, the family and the community all help build it. Inequalities between pupils inculcated in their home environments must not be allowed to translate to the classroom and perpetuate the myth of equality, so take the equitable line and support each pupil as an individual. Cultural capital is part of a wider vista that must also incorporate social and economic capital; it cannot be separate from it in your thinking as you plan to develop it. Ed Hirsch (1985, p 47) puts it well:

> *Cultural Literacy does not mean Core Curriculum ... we deprive our pupils of crucially important information if our curriculum fails to provide also the extensive information that literate people in our culture share.*

Hirsch (1985, p 47) refers to being culturally literate as having the '*basic information needed to thrive*'. Teachers and schools need to be part of the system that provides this to pupils.

Practical task for tomorrow ◄◄◄

- How diverse and inclusive is your current teaching sequence?

- What changes could you make or what references could you introduce that would celebrate some of the forgotten voices or the hidden gems?

Don't be afraid to branch away from what is the agreed 'normal' and incorporate other voices, parallel narratives, diverse faces and ideas into your teaching.

Practical task for next week ◄◄◄

As an aspect of curriculum, teachers must consider the place held by cultural capital, social knowledge and British values.

- Conduct an audit of the topic, unit or module that you are currently teaching and identify points at which these areas are explicitly addressed within the context of the subject.

- If there are noticeable gaps, how could these be filled?

- Review the opportunities you have highlighted in the first task and consider how you might weave those into the existing model.

Practical task for the longer term ◀◀◀

As you plan your sequences of teaching, make sure you are planning for progress. Consider the following prompts and use them to evaluate each sequence you design.

- How have you identified potential gaps in learning or misconceptions that pupils may be bringing into your classroom?

- What plans do you have to address those gaps?

- Is the intent of your proposed curriculum challenging enough for all pupils? Does it take into account the full breadth of pupils' existing knowledge and skills?

- Are you fully prepared to pitch your curriculum implementation to the right level for the intent?

What next? ◀ ◀ ◀

Further reading

If you are interested in looking further into some of the effects of curriculum choices, try John Hattie's research: Hattie, J (2009) *Visible Learning*. London: Routledge.

Hirsch, E (2016) *Why Knowledge Matters: Rescuing our Children from Failed Educational Theories*. Cambridge, MA: Harvard University Press.

Myatt, M (2018) *The Curriculum: Gallimaufry to Coherence*. Woodbridge: John Catt Educational.

References

Brophy, J (2000) *Teaching; Educational Practice Series 1*. Geneva: UNESCO IBE.

Cuthbert, A and Standish, A (2021) *What Should Schools Teach? Disciplines, Subjects and the Pursuit of Truth*. London: UCL Press.

Deng, Z (2022) Powerful Knowledge, Educational Potential and Knowledge-Rich Curriculum: Pushing the Boundaries. *Journal of Curriculum Studies*, 54(5): 599–617.

Department for Education (2019) *Early Career Framework*. [online] Available at: https://assets.publishing.service.gov.uk/government/uploads/system/uploads/attachment_data/file/978358/Early-Career_Framework_April_2021.pdf (accessed 15 February 2023).

Hirsch, E D Jr (1985) Cultural Literacy Doesn't Mean Core Curriculum. *The English Journal*, 74(6): 47–9.

Hummel, C E (1994) *Tyranny of the Urgent*. Westmont, IL: IVP Books.

Ofsted (2022a) *Early Inspection Framework*. [online] Available at: www.gov.uk/government/publications/education-inspection-framework/education-inspection-framework (accessed 15 February 2023).

Ofsted (2022b) *School Inspection Handbook: Part 2 – Evaluating the Quality of Education – the Curriculum*. [online] Available at: www.gov.uk/government/publications/school-inspection-handbook-eif/school-inspection-handbook#evaluating-the-quality-of-education-1 (accessed 15 February 2023).

Posner, G and Rudnitsky, A (2001) *Course Design: A Guide to Curriculum Development for Teachers*. New York: Longman.

Stenhouse, L (1975) *An Introduction to Curriculum Research and Development*. Oxford: Heinemann.

Zimmerman, B J (1989) A Social Cognitive View of Self-Regulated Academic Learning. *Journal of Educational Psychology*, 81: 329–39.

Chapter 6   Curriculum implementation 1: curriculum enactment

The provision of materials is not a sufficient condition for the attainment of curriculum development ... the hard work lies in their successful dissemination and implementation.

(Howson, 1979, p 158)

What? (The big idea) ◀◀ ◀

Implementation as the translation of intent into the classroom

The inherent challenge with all things curriculum is content coverage versus its adversary: time. Because you have to cover so much – and want to cover so much more – you will often find yourself making tough choices about what to include and what to omit, what to spend time on, what to cursorily glance at, what to reference, what to ignore. What is your core? What hinterland can you 'hint' at? The quality of classroom practice is what determines the worth of the intent and its practical translation.

From the 'what' of the intent to the 'now what' of implementation, once you know what your intentions are you can begin to plan for them to be realised: implementation is how the intentions manifest themselves in the classroom; how they are taught; how they are assessed and evaluated; what strategies will be used to ensure that biological principles of human cognitive architecture and their implications on course design are acknowledged.

The manifestation of successful implementation is twofold: what is actually happening in the classroom and how well the teachers and leaders can articulate this – there must be coherence (that word again) and calibration from intent through to this stage to ensure that all materials and processes used by classroom teachers to promote outcomes for pupils align with the 'vision' for the curriculum aspect itself; implementation is very much a 'real-world' test of the perceived intentions, and therefore requires careful thought and contextual planning. For example, if your school has a three-year Key Stage 4, why was this decision made and how does it help to implement the curriculum intent?

The focus in delivery must be on the memory, not the memories. Promote and support high-quality teaching through effective strategies, just be aware that different curriculum areas, domains, phases and topics lend themselves to being taught in different ways. The subject itself needs to shine through, and to be reflected and celebrated in the chosen pedagogical approach, otherwise that subject is homogenised and diminished by inaccurate association – physical education looks different from music; geography needs to be geographical, not just a version of an English lesson with more urban conurbations and oxbow lakes; phonics can't be taught in exactly the same way as numeracy. Allow the teaching and the content to be matched, lest you ruin both.

The successful implementation of the curriculum, however, is not just down to the teachers; what the pupils do is proof that the implementation approach taken is working (or not). It is the role of subject leaders to have the knowledge and expertise to design and monitor their individual curriculum areas, but they are all part of the greater whole.

A good place to start is with the core knowledge – the essentials, the foundations, the building blocks. We can explicitly reference the core – the threshold concepts – and then signpost what is known as the 'hinterland', the wider relevance, the deeper thinking, the broader applications.

Nuthall (2007) reminds us that learning takes time, and we are better off investing teaching time into a smaller number of what he refers to as 'big questions' in greater depth than covering every single curriculum statement in a surface level of detail – after all, a little knowledge is a dangerous thing. The further point to be aware of regarding Nuthall's seminal research is the emphasis of the experience in which the curriculum content is contained. When Nuthall and his colleagues asked pupils to recall what they remembered from classroom experiences, they found that the curriculum content was wrapped up tightly in the circumstances in which the information was encountered. For example, if pupils fill out a worksheet or complete a cloze activity, they learn that learning involves filling in the gaps in what someone else has put together; if they are listening to a lecture-style delivery, they learn that learning happens by receiving information from others in a passive way. In summary, along with the content of the curriculum, pupils learn the processes and frameworks in which that content has been embedded.

What is implementation?

There is many a slip twixt cup and lip. Intent is all very well but it is only through strong implementation that the aspirational intentions of the curriculum on paper will manifest as the desired impact for pupils. The Early Career Framework (ECF) (Department for Education, 2021) requires teachers to learn how to *deliver a carefully sequenced and coherent curriculum'*, and in doing so help those 'impact' ideals become a reality. The key consideration is that of context: your classroom space and core teaching beliefs, and fidelity to yourself while also delivering on the wider curriculum model being followed across your department, your faculty, your key stage. There are so many levels of curriculum that it resembles a family tree, a hierarchy. Each individual lesson is part of a wider picture, built in chunks of different shapes and sizes – little vignettes and episodes in the broader, sweeping, epic narrative arc. In essence, the implementation phase is the active content of the teaching or instruction process – the *what*.

A natural gap will materialise between the aspiration or prediction of the intent and the actual manifestation of the implementation; it is impossible for everything to translate. The cause of the gap is time, teacher confidence, teacher motivation and, perhaps at the root of it all, teacher subject knowledge; there is no single guidebook, framework or handbook to implementation – even of the national curriculum.

Brophy (2000) maintains that the curriculum must not be seen as an end in itself; rather, it must be considered as a means of *'helping students to learn what is considered essential for preparing them to fulfil adult roles in society and realize their potential as individuals'* (Brophy, 2000, p 14). Brophy goes on to say that the single central goal of the curriculum is learner outcomes: knowledge, skills, values, attitudes and behaviours. The curriculum exists because of its goals, so the beliefs about what is needed to accomplish those goals must guide every step in the implementation of the curriculum. Brophy wants us to ensure that all the component elements of the curriculum – content, pedagogies, tasks, assessment – are selected as means to help pupils accomplish the overall purposes laid out in the intent.

The root of the curriculum lies in the soil of cognitive science – the development of schema in pupils. The ECF (Department for Education, 2021) reminds us of this on a number of occasions within subject and curriculum knowledge. Through the lens of the science of learning, we can see that we need to be aware of the principles that underpin the following ECF statements:

> *3.3 Ensuring pupils master foundational concepts and knowledge before moving on is likely to build pupils' confidence and help them succeed.*

3.6 In order for pupils to think critically, they must have a secure understanding of knowledge within the subject area they are being asked to think critically about.

3.7 In all subject areas, pupils learn new ideas by linking those ideas to existing knowledge, organising this knowledge into increasingly complex mental models (or 'schemata'); carefully sequencing teaching to facilitate this process is important.

3.8 Pupils are likely to struggle to transfer what has been learnt in one discipline to a new or unfamiliar context.

Successful implementation requires careful thought, planning and full understanding; curricula are enacted by many, so should be planned collaboratively by all concerned to ensure that understanding is formed early and isn't just at 'surface level'. Yes, many of the concepts outlined above will have been considered in our previous stage of intent, but they have to be brought to fruition through teacher practice – as Herbert Simon said, *'learning results from what the student does and thinks, and only from what the student does and thinks; the teacher can advance learning only by influencing what the student does to learn'* (quoted in Ambrose et al, 2010, p 1).

So what?

Designing tasks with every learner in mind, orchestrated with the principles of learning science and multiple opportunities for pupils to revisit material, means we will, by default, be unequal in our coverage in terms of effectiveness. If we use the concept of the big question – those with the most impact, relevance and significance – then we, again by default but also design, subsume the smaller linked questions and ideas.

To return to Brophy (2000, p 14), pupil understanding means that *'students learn both the individual elements in a network of related content and the connections among them'* to enable them to explain content clearly, generate critical ideas and make connections to prior knowledge. Brophy also urges us to emphasise appreciation of the curriculum in our delivery – to authenticate it, to encourage pupils to value it because they believe there are good reasons for learning it. The curriculum can become the centre of the cycle for development, both within pupils and among teachers who are seeking to improve, as indicated by Figure 6.1, adapted from Ambrose et al (2010).

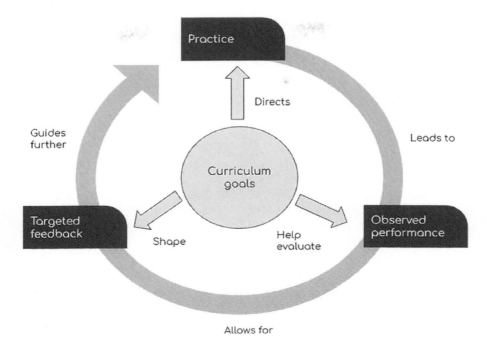

Figure 6.1 A curriculum-centred goal cycle, adapted from Ambrose et al, 2010

You create coherence: internal coherence, the connection and relationships between the taught content; and external coherence, the relationship between the intent and the various ways and contexts in which it is implemented. If curriculum is a narrative, then we have a storyline to plot – remember the analogy of the curriculum as a journey? Remember, too, the ideas of core and hinterland; there is so much wrapped up with the curriculum content – not least the instructional formats debated above – that we have to be sure we control the threads of our narrative and give each one balance, weight and a conclusion; often this is in the form of a summative, high-stakes test, but it need not be. A high-stakes, summative test such as a GCSE or an end-of-unit assessment will only ever sample and provide evidence for the understanding of a small area of the curriculum as a whole. How can you ensure that pieces of the jigsaw fit together without duplication, overlap or gaps?

The practicality of implementation is best seen as the conversion of the abstract intent concept into the concrete learning construct. You need to understand in detail the narrative of the curriculum content and what this 'looks like' in realisation – as an English teacher, I constantly question whether or not the vocabulary the pupil has used is 'sophisticated' or merely 'ambitious'; only through multiple experiences with the outcomes will I develop a better idea of what I am looking for and how it relates to my overall curriculum narrative.

Reflective task ◀◀◀

- What are the abstract concepts in your intent?

- What do they look like as concrete constructs?

All the statements within our 'intent' need to be made meaningful by orienting them within the domains in which they will be enacted – providing a context for the story to be told. Each concept needs to be brought to life, and as it is turned from concept to construct we acknowledge that they are small parts of a larger web of learning. They are not isolated knowledge, skill or understanding 'units', but instead elements to be integrated, incorporated or assimilated into existing knowledge – steps in much longer, more powerful narratives.

Determining those big ideas

Big questions can be used as a means by which the abstract concepts can be manifested into the concrete learning constructs outlined above – your curriculum can be what Ofsted (2022) would call *'focused and sequenced'*; your 'knowledge-rich' approach is one where all leaders of curriculum are clear on the 'invaluable knowledge' they want their students to acquire.

Let's look at a piece of research that may assist us: *MARGE*, by Arthur Shimamura (2018). In his seminal work, he lays out his practical suggestions for teachers tackling conceptual learning using the basis of cognitive science. He promotes the idea that we don't 'soak up' learning; instead, we use a 'top-down processing' approach whereby we actively use our existing knowledge to select relevant information.

In simple terms, the model is as follows.

M: Motivate – support pupils to generate mental motivation to focus on necessary material and avoid distraction; this can be done by stimulating curiosity through storytelling, experiences or big questions – links to over-arching schema. See the connection to the ideas of curriculum sequencing.

A: Attend – generate and sustain pupil attention by linking new ideas to existing ones and chunking material into smaller steps that build a bigger picture. Again, we've seen this before ...

R: Relate – pupils build secure schema by repeatedly relating new information to that which already exists in the said schema – the use of analogies, representations and meaningful chunks of ideas helps here.

G: Generate – pupils reframe taught content in their own words and terms, securing the material as long-lasting memories. Shimamura suggests using a range of practice and retrieval tasks here, many of which can be found in a range of sources.

E: Evaluate – pupils must use accurate supporting resources to check their own knowledge, fill gaps and differentiate between short-term performance and longer-term learning; this can be done with delayed testing, interleaving, generative testing and the use of flash cards.

The M is of interest: curriculum built on initial motivation through revealing the bigger picture to pupils at the outset, and orienting each learning episode – or set of concrete constructs – within that wider abstract framework. Shimamura asks you to consider stimulating curiosity by bringing the outside in, connecting to the 'real world' – how might you do that? Remember that all curriculum implementation must be domain specific, not generic; wholesale or single-use pedagogies employed without thought will not enable the effective manifestation of the abstract conceptual intent into concrete learning construct and practice.

Reflective task ◀◀◀

- Graham Nuthall (2007) states that effective teaching requires the teacher to allow for larger questions or problems to be broken down into smaller linked problems that are essential to solving the larger one. What might this look like for you in your subject?

- Do you know the big ideas in your topic? Can you answer the big questions yourself? If you had to list the top ten key ideas for each topic you are teaching, what would they be?

- What are the common misconceptions with this topic? How do you know they are 'common'?

- Take a forthcoming topic. Break down the 'Big Question' into a series of smaller, connected tasks for students, like a jigsaw.

Now what? ◀ ◀ ◀

We can reflect on what implications our curriculum knowledge may have by addressing a number of key questions in relation to implementation.

Practical task for tomorrow

Rate and develop: red, amber or green?

Element (adapted from Ofsted, 2022 criteria)	Now	Date of first review	Date of second review
I have good knowledge of the subject and courses I teach.			
I present subject matter clearly, promoting appropriate discussion about the subject matter being taught.			
I check pupils' understanding systematically, identify misconceptions accurately and provide clear, direct feedback.			
I respond and adapt my teaching as necessary without unnecessarily elaborate or individualised approaches.			
My teaching is designed to help pupils to remember the content they have been taught in the long term, and to integrate new knowledge into larger ideas.			
I create an environment that focuses on pupils; my chosen materials clearly support the intent of a coherently planned and sequenced curriculum.			
The work I give to pupils is demanding and matches the aims of the curriculum in being coherently planned and sequenced.			

Practical task for next week

- What blend of instructional or pedagogical approaches do you expect to see used to help pupils gain secure knowledge of [insert your topic]?

- How effectively do you keep pupils focused on the big ideas across an entire sequence of learning?

- Why have you designed the task in that way? How does that task best provide pupils with opportunities to demonstrate their understanding?

- How does the pupil response to that task provide you with evidence from which you can infer understanding?

- Are there any sensitive concepts in the sequence that need careful handling? How will they be handled?

- Which pupils may struggle with concept [X, Y, Z] and how will you mitigate/ scaffold them in that?

- What further subject-specific development do you need to effectively implement the intended curriculum?

Practical task for the longer term ◀◀◀

- Next time you are required to plan out a sequence of learning or a scheme of work, start with the big ideas – list them and reframe them as big questions to be answered.

- Map out your curriculum using each big question as the overall heading for a 'step' in the sequence, ensuring it can be answered once the step is completed – a step may comprise between one and three lessons.

- Use retrieval tasks to encourage recall of the answers to the big questions as and when they have been taught, helping to diagnose whether or not any re-teaching is required.

What next?

Further reading

The elaboration theory

Reigeluth, C and Stein, F (1983) The Elaboration Theory of Instruction. In Reigeluth, C (ed), *Instructional Design Theories and Models* (pp 367–78). Hillsdale, NJ: Lawrence Erlbaum.

Domain-specific knowledge

Tricot, A and Sweller, J (2014) Domain-specific Knowledge and Why Teaching Generic Skills Does Not Work. *Educational Psychology Review*, 26: 265–83.

Assessing intent, implementation and impact

Ofsted (2018) *An Investigation into How to Assess the Quality of Education Through Curriculum Intent, Implementation and Impact.* [online] Available at: https://assets.publishing.service. gov.uk/government/uploads/system/uploads/attachment_data/file/936097/Curriculum_ research_How_to_assess_intent_and_implementation_of_curriculum_191218.pdf (accessed 16 February 2023).

This review of the Ofsted research on curriculum is a useful guide to 'what they are looking for', particularly the different quality requirements.

References

Ambrose, S A, Bridges, M W, DiPietro, M, Lovett, M C and Norman, M K (2010) *How Learning Works: Seven Research-based Principles for Smart Teaching.* San Francisco: Jossey-Bass.

Brophy, J (2000) *Teaching; Educational Practice Series 1.* Geneva: UNESCO IBE.

Department for Education (2021) *Early Career Framework.* [online] Available at: https://assets.publishing.service.gov.uk/government/uploads/system/uploads/attachment_ data/file/978358/Early-Career_Framework_April_2021.pdf (accessed 14 February 2023).

Howson, A G (1979) A Critical Analysis of Curriculum Development in Mathematical Education. In International Commission on Mathematical (ed), *New Trends in Mathematical Teaching, Vol. IV* (pp 134–61). Paris: UNESCO.

Nuthall, G (2007) *The Hidden Lives of Learners.* Wellington: NZCER Press.

Ofsted (2022) *Schools Inspection Handbook.* [online] Available at: www.gov.uk/government/ publications/school-inspection-handbook-eif/school-inspection-handbook (accessed 14 February 2023).

Shimamura, A (2018) *MARGE – A Whole Brain Learning Approach.* [online] Available at: https://shimamurapubs.files.wordpress.com/2018/09/marge_shimamura.pdf (accessed 14 February 2023).

Chapter 7   Curriculum implementation 2: classroom level

Teachers must know the subject they teach. Indeed, there may be nothing more foundational to teacher competency. The reason is simple: Teachers who do not themselves know a subject well are not likely to have the knowledge they need to help pupils learn this content.

(Ball et al, 2008, p 404)

What? (The big idea)

You now need to consider the various pieces of the puzzle that fit together to realise successful implementation. The curriculum on paper is in reality an overview of the necessary knowledge to be imparted by teachers and learned by pupils. Each lesson plan within that sequence is an anticipation – not a concrete determinant – of what will happen. Much of the implementation of curriculum is responsive, framed by the clear parameters of the intended goals and the content. Implementation is the means of translating the intent over time into a structure and narrative within your context.

A huge part of successful implementation is acceptance that not everything in your intent will manifest as you anticipate; context remains king. Good intent statements anticipate the necessary responsiveness, building plan B into plan A.

Individual teachers operate at the classroom level; they define their classrooms through their interactions, attitudes and beliefs; therefore, they determine the effectiveness of the curriculum at point of delivery, sometimes unconsciously.

So what?

Subject-level thinking

Teachers must be proactive in their implementation of the curriculum; there is a big difference between consistency to established cultures and mere compliance with prescribed structures; the latter can lead to a reductionist approach to pedagogy as simply techniques for instruction. A good curriculum provides an education that is experienced by pupils, not simply delivered. Delivery implies that education through implementation of the curriculum is a product rather than a process. It implies transmission, as opposed to rich and varied experience.

Teachers can implement curriculum in two ways and at two levels: the level of the subject as a whole and the level of their individual classrooms. The sharing of curriculum resources and materials is a vital aspect of successful and efficient working, but it also carries a heavy caveat – one size fits one. To start with, as outlined at the beginning of this chapter, you need to know your subject and you need to know your curriculum intent. Without those foundations, you are not able to act as an informed and critical consumer of ideas, nor can you confidently make decisions at the implementation stage that help breathe life into the curriculum in the classroom.

Moreover, you mustn't forget a teacher's basic calling: helping pupils learn. The essence of pedagogy to enact curriculum is the art of creating 'community property' – making the internal external; working on knowledge with pupils and allowing them to demonstrate what they know further and more confidently.

At the subject level, you need to consider the long and medium-term plans with which you are working. Is there a clear sequence, guided by realisable goals? The key to good longer-term plans is the freedom for teachers to apply their individual pedagogical approaches and knowledge, but also remain true to the necessary content. Simplicity and clarity are key to ensuring consistency and coherence – ambiguity breeds anarchy. These plans should be straightforward and as brief as possible – it is far easier for everyone to be on the same page if there is only one page from which to work.

Designing instruction

Now we need to look more directly at the instruments and mechanisms of curriculum implementation, focusing on our two favourite 'eff' words – efficiency and effectiveness. When time and content coverage are two conflicting aspects of delivery, teachers have to do the right things, and do them in the right way and at the right time.

According to the Early Career Framework (ECF) (Department for Education, 2021), the following strategies are necessary to support students to build increasingly complex mental models.

>> Discuss curriculum design with experienced colleagues and balancing exposition, repetition, practice of critical skills and knowledge.

>> Revisit the big ideas of the subject over time and teaching key concepts through a range of examples.

>> Draw explicit links between new content and the core concepts and principles in the subject.

First, you must consider the 'shape' of the journey that pupils will undertake. For example, research indicates very clearly that a curriculum built on the principles of spaced practice as opposed to blocked approaches, utilising the power of retrieval, will yield more positive outcomes for pupils. Spacing and retrieval are defined as follows (Sharples et al, 2018):

>> *spaced learning* – distributing learning and retrieval opportunities over a longer period of time rather than concentrating them in 'massed' practice;

>> *retrieval practice* – using a variety of strategies to recall information from memory, for example flash cards, practice tests or quizzing, or mind-mapping.

Showing pupils the relationships between past learning and present learning increases the breadth and depth of what they are learning. Teachers need to design learning experiences that help pupils to not only benefit from this but also understand why it is important. Pupils can develop their own metacognitive approaches through a greater understanding of the principles of effective learning, giving them some choice in their learning goals and teaching them to be attentive to their progress and processes yields learning gains.

According to Carpenter et al (2022, p 496): *'Effective learning skills are critical for navigating an increasingly complex world.'* There are *'important implications [for curriculum design] for the increasingly common situations in which the learners must effectively monitor and regulate their own learning'*.

Carpenter et al (2022, p 497) see spacing as *'when to engage in learning'* and retrieval as part of a plan for *'how to learn effectively'*. They go on to tell us that, for pupils to build sturdy, durable knowledge, they have to *'repeatedly study and use the information that they are trying to learn'*. The timing of this is vital, but it is often not considered significantly enough: *'repeated practice opportunities that are spaced apart in time are more effective than the same number of practice opportunities that occur closer together.'*

For example, Key Stage 1 pupils learning basic scientific principles benefited hugely from a spaced approach of one lesson a day across four days when compared with their peers who received a massed approach (Carpenter et al, 2022). Key Stage 3 pupils evaluating websites are more effective learners if their lessons are scheduled a week apart as opposed to a day apart, and Key Stage 4 pupils perform better than their peers on physics problems when each practice problem is spaced apart by one day.

As teachers, you must ensure that important curriculum content – in particular those essential concepts from which connections stem – is reviewed and revisited; delayed review has a large positive impact on the amount of material that can be remembered later. Practically, we need to be sure we have enough spacing, and not worry about having too much. Finding space for spacing isn't hard either – build review into the daily diet of the classroom through simple techniques such as 'last term, last month, last week' questions, explicitly narrating connections to previous material. Also consider the power of homework as a tool for creating more space in the taught curriculum – pupils can review and consolidate previously taught material at home, providing this is followed up in classrooms.

Above all, pupils need to know why they are always reviewing material and why it is okay to forget – it may be that you see substantial forgetting at the outset of a spacing approach. Instead of being discouraged, though, research has shown that reawakening of the taught knowledge through retrieval and review is more easily accomplished than the original learning was, and that the final result is a marked reduction in the rate of forgetting. By using spacing, you can not only repair the forgetting that might have happened since the initial learning stage, but inoculate against any subsequent forgetting.

A well-implemented curriculum will provide multiple opportunities for pupils to review and revisit previously taught material, embedding it into long-term memory and strengthening schema. For example, graphic organisers, textbooks and other scaffolds all have their place if they are used well and pupils see their value; too often, rushed or shallow implementation is the key cause of ineffective impact.

Reflective task ◀◀◀

- What does your classroom look like, and what does it sound like? Are you creating the most supportive environment for learning that promotes interactions and relationships between pupils based on respect and empathy?

- Are you maximising their opportunity to learn by being efficient with time and resources?

- Are your instructions clear so pupils understand what they are doing and, importantly, why?

- Are you catering for all of your pupils and their various needs?

- How much of the lesson do you model and lead, and how much do pupils engage with?

- How do you orient your pupils within the wider curriculum to ensure connections are forged and strengthened?

- Do you use a range of peer opportunities for reflection, improvement, discussion and oracy?

- Do you promote literacy within your subject, domain or phase to help broaden the pupil in the wider world?

- Do you provide opportunities to enrich the cultural capital of pupils and embrace diversity?

- Do your teaching sequences activate hard thinking within pupils through explaining, modelling, questioning, interacting and embedding? (Coe et al, 2019)

Lesson planning

At classroom level, you think about how you translate long and medium-term plans into shorter sequences and the individual lessons that constitute them. You look at your own competencies and beliefs, your strengths and areas to develop, and your confidence with the material. You *know your pupils*, so you can adapt and scaffold accordingly. You present, process and model the curriculum, but it is the pupils who must learn it. A good lesson plan is the anticipation of expected events in the classroom, not the determinant; however, with more experience each time, you can mitigate against the anticipated negative outcomes and ensure that your choices of task – and the way you design the task – will allow pupils the opportunity to demonstrate how much of the curriculum they have learnt at that point.

Individual lesson plans are always part of a wider sequence. They are the tactics used to enact the overall strategy; they do not exist in a vacuum and they do not start to 'manifest' the moment the pupils enter the room – there is what comes before and what must come after (see Figure 7.1).

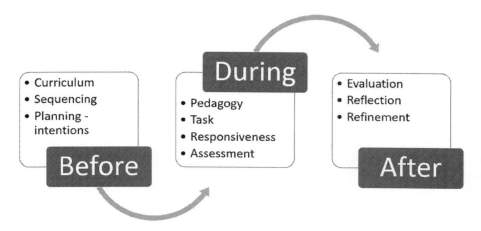

- Curriculum
- Sequencing
- Planning - intentions

Before

During

- Pedagogy
- Task
- Responsiveness
- Assessment

- Evaluation
- Reflection
- Refinement

After

Figure 7.1 A lesson plan as part of a series of thoughts

The act of planning takes place in a far quieter and more reflective environment than teaching – planning allows you to make *more intentional changes to your practice*. In short, planning makes it possible. No lesson plan survives its first encounter with a pupil, so much of what you hope might happen is confounded by the realities of the changeable and unpredictable nature of the environment. However, habits of thought and practice wisdom help to make planning a positive process. You must focus on the active verb, not the static noun.

Although a single lesson plan is not the best way to plan a lesson, you can apply principles to the planning of short sequences and teaching bursts that move pupils from one milestone to another in the most efficient way possible: where are they now, where do they need to be, how will we know if they've got there, how can I help them? Planning, teaching and assessment are all interlinked and all, like the wider curriculum, are organic – not static.

The key is to remember that teachers teach and pupils learn; therefore, the plan for the lesson needs to best facilitate learning experiences to optimise the possibilities of retention – the plan is for the teacher, not the pupil.

Lessons must accommodate principles of cognition and learning science, psychology, emotions, mindset and much more – the art, craft and science of teaching is to present the curriculum in such a way as to make it palatable to the tastes of all pupils. Planning, however, is not just a competency – it is a skill; it needs content – factual subject knowledge – before it can be commenced. You can't plan with nothing.

Planning is a task that takes time, and this must be factored into the curriculum itself; shared resources can be useful, as can textbooks, but you must be aware of the potential limitations of the off-the-shelf resource! Planning is visualising the enactment of the curriculum, anticipating the likely outcomes and actions but not always predicting them accurately. In short, effective planning anticipates what *might* happen with more accuracy each time, and therefore implements the intended curriculum more effectively.

You can arouse curiosity about curriculum content in your pupils as a way of motivating them to attend; you can enrich their awareness of abstract concepts by providing multiple and frequent worked and real-world examples; you can assess their progress in a range of ways, but the following are some core aspects that must be adhered to if you are to successfully implement the curriculum at classroom level.

» Prior knowledge is a vital aspect of learning anything new – curriculum content should be introduced on the foundation of existing ideas.

» Apparently, the road to hell is paved with good intentions, but it is also the road to an effective lesson, providing you are happy to deviate if necessary. Set up lessons with clear intentions linked to curriculum goals, and with supporting tasks that help exemplify pupil understanding (see below).

» Planning is a load in itself; every moment spent planning a lesson is a moment that might be spent elsewhere; keep it simple, keep it efficient – what is the minimum your pupils need to do to make progress?

» High short-term performance can often be a mask for longer-term effective learning; curriculum implementation must create stable structures, not wobbly ones.

» Transitions between phases of lessons help to determine perceived lesson 'pace'. A 'punchy' lesson can be achieved with fewer instructions and explanations and more structured routines and straightforward tasks.

» Effective learning – the goal of all curriculum implementation – is achieved through desirable difficulties. Effective learning needs to include explicit opportunities to connect new knowledge to existing knowledge in meaningful ways, rather than just playing around with concepts in a shallow way – learning requires effort.

» Tasks must be designed as an agreement between pupil and teacher to demonstrate a shared understanding. Tasks that don't allow pupils to demonstrate taught content as intended can be anachronistic and incongruous; they can even be damaging. A good example is asking a pupil to design a newspaper front page to illustrate their understanding of the events of the Battle of Hastings. Yes, there will be related content, but the pupil must also recall key features of a newspaper front page (not relevant to the learning) and also embrace the idea that mass-print media existed in 1066 (misconception and anachronism). Task design is vital, and it must be done properly.

» Be flexible so you can be responsive; beware the lure of the sacrosanct sub-folder for each lesson or the timings on a lesson plan – these can bind and restrict you, hampering your ability to adapt if the need arises. Try using a slide deck instead of a sub-folder, shifting content up and down as opposed to sticking to a finite and non-negotiable end-point for every individual lesson.

A key word in a lot of the above is 'meaningful': pupils need to see concepts as valid, authentic and worthwhile.

Implementation is massive – there is no doubt about that. The best development for your own understanding of effective implementation is to view it through a subject or phase lens. What are the core curriculum concepts in your area and what are the most effective pedagogies for manifesting them?

Observation of more experienced practitioners – with a clear focus – is the best way to develop your own practice in your subject or phase.

Now what?

Practical task for tomorrow

- What learning routines are currently evident in your classroom?

- Why do you have them, and how do they help to maximise learning for your pupils?

- Make a list of the routines and processes you expect a pupil to go through in one of your lessons tomorrow, and why you want them to do it. An example is provided below.

Routine	Reason
Lining up quietly outside the classroom before entering.	To create a settled sense of order and allow me to control the entry to the learning environment, indicating the initial activity as pupils enter.

Practical task for next week ◀◀◀

Now you have reviewed your routines, you can reflect on your planning – too often we spend too much time planning at the detriment of considering our delivery and responsiveness.

- Try to write down your typical 'lesson structure'.

- What are the standard phases of a 'normal' lesson that you teach, and why does each phase exist?

This may be easier if you reflect on a number of lessons in the same sequence and get a sense of 'best fit' (see the example below).

Phase	Reason
1 Pupils enter and engage in my 'do now' task.	The 'do now' task acts as an opportunity for me to review relevant previous content and set up the next stage of the sequence, as well acting as a settler.

Practical task for the longer term ◀◀◀

As discussed above, task design is so important in ensuring that pupils engage in activities that allow them to demonstrate what they have learnt. Their responses to tasks indicate to you what they have interpreted from your teaching.

- Keep a log of the different tasks you ask pupils in your lessons to complete – for example, a gap-fill, a worksheet, a concept map, practice questions.

- Evaluate their effectiveness against the learning intentions of the lesson itself – was it the best task for the job?

What next? ◀ ◀ ◀

Further reading

Sherrington, T and Caviglioli, O (2020) *Teaching Walkthrus: Five-step Guides to Instructional Coaching.* Woodbridge: John Catt Educational. This book further elaborates on implementation at classroom level.

References

Ball, D, Thames, M and Phelps, G (2008) Content Knowledge for Teaching: What Makes It Special? *Journal of Teacher Education*, 59(5). https://doi.org/10.1177/002248710 8324554.

Carpenter, S, Pan, S and Butler, A (2022) The Science of Effective Learning with Spacing and Retrieval Practice. *National Review of Psychology* 1: 496–511.

Coe, R, Rauch, C, Kime, S and Singleton, D (2019) *Great Teaching Toolkit: Evidence Review.* Evidence Based Education. [online] Available at: https://assets.website-files.com/ 5ee28729f7b4a5fa99bef2b3/5ee9f507021911ae35ac6c4d_EBE_GTT_EVIDENCE% 20REVIEW_DIGITAL.pdf (accessed 14 February 2023).

Department for Education (2021) *Early Career Framework.* [online] Available at: https://assets.publishing.service.gov.uk/government/uploads/system/uploads/attachment_ data/file/978358/Early-Career_Framework_April_2021.pdf (accessed 14 February 2023).

Sharples, J, Albers, B and Fraser, S (2018) *Putting Evidence to Work: A School's Guide to Implementation.* London: Education Endowment Foundation.

Chapter 8   Curriculum implementation 3: assessing the curriculum

What? (The big idea) ◀◀◀

If teaching is the manifestation of the curriculum in practice through pedagogy, then assessment is the tool that validates your teaching of the curriculum against the established goals – the bridge between teaching and learning, as Dylan Wiliam (2014) puts it. Assessment validates the curriculum; it does not guide it. The curriculum exists through the interactions and relationships between teacher and pupil, with assessment strategies monitoring the journey between the milestones.

It must be acknowledged that one test fits few; assessment is designed on the basis of the evidence the assessor wishes to elicit, and in turn what decisions are made based on that evidence. Research and investigation into adaptive teaching would suggest that teachers need to understand that inclusion doesn't operate solely in the realm of support teams, but in fact is in the hands of the classroom teacher. Is the test fit for purpose for all? You should consider the empathetic application of adaptive strategies to support learning for all your pupils. Assessment, in all its form, can really help here. By actively monitoring the implementation of your curriculum through various assessment strategies, you will be able to determine what is being learnt and by whom, and what needs to be taught next.

So what? ◀◀◀

Assessing progress through the curriculum

There is no occupation in which the workers must change jobs every fifty minutes, move to another location, and work under the direction of another supervisor. Yet this is precisely what we ask of adolescents, hoping, at the same time, to provide them with a coherent educational program.
(Eisner, 2005, p 142)

A curriculum is a force of nature; it is never static, and will either grow and flourish if it is well tended, or wither and decay if it is neglected. You would never knowingly or deliberately give someone the wrong directions, nor would you send them down a road you knew to be a dead end. You wouldn't expect someone to keep driving towards a road closure, but nor would you let a pupil carry on towards an obvious misconception. Would you start doing something, keep at it for 12 years and then be happy to be told you had failed? No. That's where formative assessment comes in. Monitoring, supporting and guiding pupils towards agreed goals, using a range of means, is an essential aspect of the implementation of the curriculum.

Teachers assess all the time, and this is essential for the monitoring of curriculum implementation; you assess to diagnose problems, identify misconceptions, determine understanding, check for completion – all the functions of a lesson; you also assess weekly, monthly, each term and topic by topic. You conduct baseline assessment before starting a topic or a unit, mid-point assessments to get a summative sense of progress and at the end of the unit to determine how much has been learnt, or at least retained.

Principles of learning science might suggest that you should use an interleaved or spaced approach to end-of-topic testing as well – check for longer-term learning as opposed to shorter-term performance by interspersing sequences with more in-depth assessments on previously taught content, as opposed to the immediate topic of study.

Brophy (2000, p 352) tells us that:

> A well-developed curriculum includes strong and functional assessment components. These assessment components are aligned with the curriculum's goals, and so they are integrated with its content, instructional methods and learning activities, and designed to evaluate progress towards its major intended outcomes.

The importance of successful and effective formative assessment strategies in our classrooms cannot be overlooked. Assessment allows you to proactively and constantly monitor the progress of pupils towards their goals – your role as a classroom teacher is to provide up-to-the-minute information about where pupils are going, how they getting there and how well they are managing their journey.

First-hand evidence of implementation comes in the form of pupil work, with their books ideally reflecting their progression across a key stage (not a single lesson – you can't demonstrate progress in a single lesson). Pupils need regular formative feedback to authenticate and validate your assessment, and to set clear targets for 'what next', 'where next' and 'how next'; yet again, a multitude of moving parts must synchronise in order to ensure effective implementation. As with every decision you make as a teacher, you need to know your *why* as well as your *what* and your *how*.

Reflective task ◀◀◀

Considering the role that effective assessment can play in your successful implementation of the intended curriculum, think about the following.

- What does assessment 'look like' in your subject/phase?

- What is assessed, by whom and when? Why is it assessed?

- How and why is feedback given, and what is done with it by pupils to advance the curriculum experience?

The quality of inferences you can make regarding the material you assess is highly dependent on the quality of the material itself and how best it demonstrates pupils' understanding of core curriculum concepts. For example, how you teach to enable pupils to understand the concepts affects how valid your assessment of the understanding of those concepts is. Do you present material clearly, promoting discussion and debate? Do you identify and offset misconceptions from the outset or do you let them manifest and then react to them? Do you give appropriate time for guided and supported practice of key concepts?

Formative assessment to inform continued implementation

In *Principled Assessment Design*, Dylan Wiliam (2014) argues that, as assessment is the servant of the curriculum and not its master, different assessments should have different roles: more formal assessment procedures should be focused on the big ideas of the curriculum, and then the 'leftovers' are dealt with more informally, following the logic of a learning pathway (or pathways) taken by pupils to reach the understanding of the core concept. These informal assessments take the form of the 'formative assessment' strategies we can explore, always on the basis that there must be a reason for each one to be used.

Formative assessments – and indeed the summative processes at the end of a sequence of learning – are only as good as the sequence they are there to validate. If there is no logical rhyme or reason for elements to be arranged in the order in which they manifest in classrooms, then the very authenticity of the assessment is called into question; only assess when you need to, and when it will inform next steps for you as a teacher and your pupils. The sequence in which assessments are utilised is entirely subject to the local context and the school itself; even with multi-academy trusts (MATs) of similar locale, we cannot assume identical pupil journeys.

The uniqueness of the pupil profile and the individual classroom allows for the exploration of the hinterland around the big ideas, but no curriculum model should stipulate exactly what these should be; these are the nuggets of gold, discovered through exploration and perhaps entirely isolated from the big ideas in all but the loosest of contexts – so embrace them!

The key ingredients of formative assessment (Wiliam, 2013, p 16) are:

1. *clarifying, sharing and understanding learning intentions;*

2. *eliciting evidence of learning;*

3. *providing feedback that feeds forwards;*

4. *activating students as learning resources for each other;*

5. *activating students as owners of their own learning.*

Each of these comes with its own bank of strategies, but the guiding principle is that the assessment is regular, useful and low-stakes; a wealth of literature, research and advice exists that can help you develop your assessment, so we do not need to go into detail here.

The bottom line, as Wiliam (2013, p 20) puts it, is that *'as long as teachers continue to investigate that extraordinary relationship between "what did I do as a teacher?" and "what did my students learn?", good things are likely to happen'.*

Reflective task ◀◀◀

Give an example from your own teaching for each question below.

- How do you know that *all* your pupils are able to access the taught curriculum?

- How do you differentiate and scaffold your teaching to meet the needs of all pupils?

- How do you identify and remedy gaps in pupils' knowledge in your classes?

- How does your implementation of the curriculum allow pupils the opportunity to revisit and review previously taught material?

- How do you formatively assess pupils' progress through the curriculum, and how is this communicated to pupils, so they have some control of their learning?

- How do you give feedback and what responses do you anticipate?

Feedback for progress

Curriculum is teaching; it is the content, the purpose of that content and the delivery of that content, coupled with the receipt of that content and the demonstration of understanding within the agreed model of 'success'.

As it is active and ever-evolving, the presence of feedback as a curricula instrument for progress is vital – without knowing how well they are doing or whether they are going in the right direction, pupils will not benefit from the riches of the practice they undertake. To give an example, a pupil who heads off into the depths of the curriculum with an embedded misconception will be harder to reel in and correct later down the line, as there is further to travel back to the correct starting point, to take the correct turn. The Early Career Framework (ECF) (Department for Education, 2021, p 12) tells us that *anticipating common misconceptions within particular subjects is an important aspect of curricular knowledge*' and the anticipation is only the start – once we anticipate, we must adjust and act accordingly; our implementation of the curriculum depends on managing the efficiency of the pupil journey.

We can argue that whether or not assessment is 'formative' or 'summative' depends largely on the feedback given and then the intentions for use of that feedback by the pupils. Evaluative feedback tells us something about the quality of a product or service; we can refer to this type of feedback as summative because it summarises all aspects of an experience. On the other hand, formative feedback is better when it indicates one aspect of the experience; such feedback is usually provided verbally rather than in writing, to make it less 'formal', less 'high-stakes'. Assessment loops will tell us (and our pupils) where they are now, where they need to get to and how they are going to get there – in essence, whether they are on track in the curriculum journey and what further guidance they might need.

The ECF (Department for Education, 2021) makes the following points about assessment and feedback.

» To be of value, teachers use information from assessments to inform the decisions they make; in turn, pupils must be able to act on feedback for it to have an effect.

» High-quality feedback can be written or verbal; it is likely to be accurate and clear, encourage further effort and provide specific guidance on how to improve.

» Over time, feedback should support pupils to monitor and regulate their own learning.

A famous analogy is that formative feedback is akin to a good murder because it requires motive (the pupil needs and wants it), opportunity (the pupil is given time to use it) and means (the pupil is able and willing to use it). When using assessment formatively to help you maintain momentum through your curriculum portrayal, you should use the following guidelines.

» *Lay the foundation.* Ensure feedback is prefaced with high-quality instruction and appropriate formative assessment strategies (see above). High-quality initial instruction actually reduces the work feedback needs to do, as the assessment strategies will set the learning intentions and assess gaps – feedback aims for the former and addresses the latter.

» *Design the right task(s).* Anachronous or meaningless tasks will render feedback void – why spend time offering strategies for improving something that was worthless to begin with?

» *Consider the timing.* There is no 'perfect time' that works every time; sometimes the pragmatist realises early on that promising to give feedback the next day causes too much of a burden and compromises the quality of the feedback produced. Instead, you should trust yourself to judge whether feedback needs to be immediate or whether you can delay it, depending on the context of the class, the characteristics of the task or the individual pupils.

» *Focus forward.* Your feedback should target specific gaps in learning or curriculum content that you have identified through your assessment, avoiding personal feedback that may hinder pupils' self-efficacy, blind them with labels or – perhaps worse – pacify them with meaningless, vague platitudes. Instead, focus on task, subject or self-regulation.

Are they ready to receive?

Pupils need to understand the purpose of feedback in relation to their access to the curriculum and your continued successful implementation of it – prepare them for this by addressing what Carless and Boud (2018) called their '*feedback literacy*': do they understand what they are being told?

Too often in teaching, the – perfectly excusable – error is made of dumbing down the assessment criteria for tasks into 'pupil friendly' versions that may actually detract from the authenticity of the assessment. If assessment serves curriculum, by diluting the assessment you detract from the curriculum. Teachers should look to educate pupils in the language of the curriculum and use this shared language to explore and guide the goals and intentions they establish, and the terminology and expression they use in their feedback. In this way, the curriculum remains at the centre of the experience. For example, focusing pupils' feedback on command words in their subject – describe, evaluate, explore, explain – can be very useful. Teach the word and its meaning, reinforce through examples and models, then target feedback around whether or not the 'command' has been met. Just as each domain is different, so too is the nuance of the command or instruction. Pupils do not have a general part of their brain that does all their analysis; rather, they use analysis in different subjects in different ways, each with their own unique approach and necessary prerequisite domain knowledge.

In the same way that simply telling pupils to 'think' won't help them to actually think, nor will the act of 'giving feedback' automatically improve pupils' grades – the onus is on them to act. For this to occur, the teacher must provide a script and a rehearsal space. The feedback therefore closes the loop. Pupils need to be literate enough in feedback to see it as a windscreen, not a rear-view mirror; simply improving their last piece of work is not sufficient – they need to do something similar better next time, and all subsequent times as they re-encounter curriculum concepts with increasing complexity. *'For feedback processes to be enhanced, pupils need both appreciation of how feedback can operate effectively and opportunities to use feedback within the curriculum'* (Carless and Boud, 2018, p 1315).

Now what?

Ensure that your formative assessment and feedback are purposeful, and that they directly support your implementation of the curriculum at classroom level. Consider the following aspects.

>> Create and share learning intentions and expectations with pupils, underpinned by exemplification of what success looks like, so pupils are capable of emulating it.

>> Diagnose and then remedy. Don't let misconceptions fester – use a range of examples and non-examples to strengthen the boundaries of concepts in the memory of pupils.

>> Support pupils to recognise gaps in understanding as they grapple with more complex concepts.

>> Provide information on *how* pupils can get to their next milestone, and *what* activities might improve performance.

>> Develop metacognition in pupils through scaffolding, support and guidance.

>> Give feedback that is focused on task, subject or self-regulation, *not* individual pupils themselves.

>> Build time into your curriculum planning – and therefore your sequences of instruction – for pupils to be made literate in, have access to and respond to feedback.

Practical task for tomorrow ◀◀◀

- Look ahead to a lesson you have planned to teach tomorrow. How are you assessing pupils and how are you giving them feedback?

Assessment	Reason	Feedback	Response
Retrieval quiz on Tudor monarchs	Checking for declarative knowledge before creating timeline	Pupils self-check answers followed by verbal feedback	Pupils correct any errors immediately to move forward with accurate information

Practical task for next week ◀◀◀

Assessments have to be both valid (worthy of the inferences you draw from them) and reliable (trustworthy in what they report). Assessment is an essential tool for successful curriculum implementation, but it must be used in the right places and at the right times. It is also important to remember the trade-off: all assessment needs feedback, and some feedback requires marking, but marking takes time.

- What are your current plans for marking pupils' books next week?

- Why?

- What response will you expect?

You might like to use a table like the one below to help with your answers.

Group	Marking because ...	Pupils will respond by ...
Year 2	Pupils have covered background information about the Stone Age	Completing the extra sentences I will put in their books, showing me that they can use their own knowledge

If you find you are marking for a reason that doesn't align with the intended curriculum, or that you are not giving pupils time to respond, revisit your reasons.

Practical task for the longer term

Homework can be a powerful tool for developing pupils' ability to practise using previously taught material, and also to develop their self-regulatory and metacognitive abilities.

- When and why do you provide opportunities for pupils to complete independent homework tasks, and what feedback do you give?

- Consider the use of homework as an opportunity for pupils to embed and consolidate what they have learned in class, and keep a log of what you set, why you set it and what it tells you about their progress.

Remember, homework shouldn't be 'new' knowledge or skills, and must be set with equity in mind.

What next?

Further reading

These texts further elaborate on assessing the curriculum as part of curriculum implementation:

Finch, A (2019) *Essential Guides for Early Career Teachers: Assessment*. St Albans: Critical Publishing.

Hattie, J and Timperley, H (2007) The Power of Feedback. *Review of Educational Research*, 77(1): 81–112.

Jones, K (2021) *Wiliam & Leahy's Five Formative Assessment Strategies in Action*. Woodbridge: John Catt Educational.

Kluger, A and DeNisi, A (1996) The Effects of Feedback Interventions on Performance: A Historical Review, a Meta-Analysis, and a Preliminary Feedback Intervention Theory. *Psychological Bulletin*, 119: 254–84.

Wiliam, D (2006) *Inside the Black Box*. London: GL Assessment.

References

Brophy, J (2000) *Teaching: Educational Practice Series 1.* Geneva: UNESCO IBE.

Carless, D and Boud, D (2018) The Development of Student Feedback Literacy: Enabling Uptake of Feedback. *Assessment & Evaluation in Higher Education*, 43: 1315–25.

Department for Education (2021) *Early Career Framework.* [online] Available at: https://assets.publishing.service.gov.uk/government/uploads/system/uploads/attachment_data/file/978358/Early-Career_Framework_April_2021.pdf (accessed 14 February 2023).

Eisner, E W (2005) *Reimagining Schools: The Selected Works of Elliot W Eisner.* London: Routledge.

Wiliam, D (2013) Assessment: The Bridge Between Teaching and Learning. *Voices from the Middle*, 21(2): 15–20.

Wiliam, D (2014) *Principled Assessment Design.* London: SSAT.

Chapter 9   Curriculum impact: what are the outcomes?

Introduction

The last great 'I' of the curriculum triumvirate is impact; what you intend, and how you implement it, is ultimately measured by the outcomes – the impact. This is the means of evaluating what knowledge and understanding pupils have gained against the expectations we had.

If we see curriculum as a product, then the impact is simply how effective our delivery of that product was – did everyone get what they wanted or expected? If we consider – as we should – curriculum as a process, then the impact must be regarded in terms of the length of the journey travelled so far, and how far there is still to go – a milestone, if you will.

To look more closely, Ofsted (2022) sees impact in the following terms.

Impact

Learners develop detailed knowledge and skills across the curriculum and, as a result, achieve well. Where relevant, this is reflected in results from national tests and examinations that meet government expectations, or in the qualifications obtained.

Learners are ready for the next stage of education, employment or training. Where relevant, they gain qualifications that allow them to go on to destinations that meet their interests, aspirations and the intention of their course of study. They read widely and often, with fluency and comprehension.

In the simplest terms, have pupils learnt what they have been taught and, perhaps more importantly, how do you know? In school-wide terms, the impact judgement feeds into the single 'quality of education' judgement, triangulating impact with intent and implementation.

What? (the big idea)

There are very simple measures for determining the impact of the curriculum at a data level.

» Does the curriculum lead to good results?

» How do those results compare with national averages?

As a classroom teacher, your impact is indeed measured with your results and your contribution to the data dashboard; in turn, that reflects in the way your performance is judged. You want nothing more than to provide the pupils in your classes with the best possible outcomes, the most progress possible – they all have data targets at key milestones and you want them to achieve and exceed them. However, the impact is the end arrived at only by the means, and not the other way round – you can't justify perceived poor outcomes by claiming highly effective implementation of another kind, nor can you dodge facts; pupils must be given the chance to meet their targets and questions are asked if they don't – in harsh terms, children have only one chance at education, and teachers are that chance.

However, measurement of the curriculum's impact should not be seen solely in such brutally quantitative terms – for example, how is it possible to accurately claim that learning over the duration of the chosen model has indeed been supplied with appropriate levels of challenge or cultural enrichment? Ofsted, for example, is not looking solely at externally verified data and results, but instead at wider-ranging indicators of that 'broad and balanced' curriculum: pupils' work in classrooms and their books; pupils' attitudes to learning and their views. Internal data is not a source of evidence, but the inferences and therefore the decisions made based on the data can be: once again, why is it collected if it is not used?

The key determinant for the impact of the curriculum is the extent to which it has reached its initial goals. Have all pupils 'accessed' it at the anticipated level? Have all pupils realised their potential?

In essence, what are the right end-points? Indeed, when does the curriculum actually end for the pupils? If it is, as argued previously, an organic and natural construct, then the seeds it has sown will continue to bloom and grow themselves, enriching and informing the next stages of learner development.

Ultimately, you can do nothing about the impact in retrospect; every system is perfectly designed to get the results it gets, and if those results are not as desired or expected, then the only thing that can be done is to return to the start of the cycle and reconsider its intent and its implementation – where did the plans come unstuck? This is why curriculum can never be a static, completed product or process. By its very nature, it is fully responsive.

Impact has to be more than just outcomes – it has to be more human than that. So, what does impact consist of? An inspection of a curriculum will balance the summative data with the more day-to-day standard of student work – they are keen to see that learning in schools must build towards a goal, and that pupils are being prepared for the next stage of their education or development. When considering evaluating your own impact, be aware that the progress of pupils towards goals is a slow, non-linear and individual process; never view any individual feedback on a single observed learning encounter as an indictment on your ability to implement curriculum over time.

Goals can be scored and promises are often broken; a curriculum is a journey towards a set of achievable goals, not a set of pie-in-the-sky promises – it is really important to see impact not as the end of the line, but as a checkpoint. It can inform next steps, as well as helping you to evaluate what has gone before.

So what? ◀ ◀ ◀

At the heart of curriculum making is the process of interpreting and unpacking the meaning and significance of the content to unlock its educational potential.

(Deng, 2022, p 610)

Tools for evaluation of impact

Impact is not just a case of *what*, but also *when*; following on from the ideas of formative assessment, you are continually gaining information on the progress your pupils are making. So *when* you put the marker in the sand is key – you can easily choose the checkpoints that give you the information you want, and you can choose the measure to make the ambition become the perceived reality. However, this is disingenuous and does everyone a disservice. You have to evaluate the actual reality, otherwise you can never be sure that the decisions you make in response to your diagnoses are the right ones.

You need to evaluate the effectiveness of the curriculum design (intent), the effectiveness of how it is taught (implementation) and not only the pupils' outcomes but also the pace at which they travelled through the content and how prepared they are for the next stage of their development. Impact is complex, nuanced and – in places – abstract and qualitative. In its published research, Ofsted (2018, p 8) uses the following statements:

The curriculum is successfully implemented to ensure pupils' progression in knowledge – pupils successfully 'learn the curriculum'.

The curriculum provides parity for all groups of pupils.

The likelihood is that, no matter how carefully constructed, meticulous, adaptive and effective the implementation is, the impact will not be an exact replica of the intent. It will – as learning is at all stages – be an interpretation of what was intended and then taught. There are many filters through which the generic, big ideas of an intended curriculum must pass before their impact is assessed.

So, as a classroom teacher on the 'front line', what are the best tools to give the best measures?

Measuring or tracking?

First, what are you measuring? What is the main determinant of impact – and successful impact at that? If you didn't know this when you started out, then you travelled blind and so did your pupils; you can't guide pupils to unknown destinations. Your curriculum knowledge is one of your key tools, so be prepared to use it wisely.

There are some other questions you can then ask yourself:

>> Was the specified amount of content covered in the allocated time, and at the appropriate pace?

>> Did all pupils demonstrate equitable outcomes in line with starting points?

>> Was the experience of the implementation fulfilling and enriching for all concerned, including the teachers delivering it?

>> Are pupils ready for their next steps? Are they prepared?

The last question is the key – the goal of the curriculum is the development of the individual.

Thus, you are called back to your intent and our design – it is possible for a student to spend 12 years in formal educational settings and still be seen to have 'failed' at the end of it. That's not right.

So what can you 'measure' and where can you find the evidence – the 'ocular proof'? If you have been using your formative assessment and feedback well during the implementation of the curriculum, there won't be any surprises. What you must not do is assume that impact can only be determined at the very end of a prescribed unit or curriculum topic – you are looking for (and feeling the effects of) implementation at all stages: in interactions with pupils, in pupils' interaction with the content and in the feelings of self-efficacy manifesting both in the pupils you teach and you as the teacher.

However, physical evidence on impact can be drawn from a range of sources.

>> *Book scrutiny* – for example, does the use of a carousel of specialisms in Key Stage 3 Design and Technology expose students to an appropriate range of disciplines for the right amount of time?

>> *Deep-dive into assessment within domains* – are there a range of clearly identifiable scaffolds and templates for formative assessment?

>> *Lesson observation* – are you ensuring that all pupils have equitable access to curriculum content, supported by appropriate strategies and interventions?

>> *Data 'drops'* – does the data suggest that pupils are making progress towards their agreed targets?

>> *Intervention initiatives* – do struggling pupils who are identified by the data or by more qualitative measures receive appropriate support to close the gap between current performance and anticipated outcomes?

>> *Teaching teams* – are you teaching in your specialist domain – subject or phase – thereby ensuring that pupils have the best expertise and instruction? If not, are you supported in developing your pedagogical content knowledge (PCK) for your other subject(s)?

It must always be remembered that all assessment (of which impact is a form) is only as good as the validity, accuracy and authenticity of the evidence from which those inferences are drawn.

Impact is the tangible (and sometimes intangible) result of what came before; at a classroom level, the impact of your implementation can be observed first hand in students' workbooks and portfolios, their coursework and classwork, their grades and test scores.

However, many impacts are felt longer term; the impact of Covid-19 lockdowns hitting the United Kingdom in March 2020, for example, is only just being properly felt – learning is a long-term process, and short-term observation doesn't provide the greatest clarity.

Brophy (2000, p 18) suggests teachers need to take the following actions to enable pupils to construct meaningful knowledge that they can access and use in their lives outside school:

(i) *retreat from breadth of coverage in order to allow time to develop the most important content in greater depth;*

(ii) *represent this important content as networks of connected information structured around powerful ideas;*

(iii) *develop the content with a focus on explaining these important ideas and the connections among them; and*

(iv) *follow up with authentic learning activities and assessment measures that provide students with opportunities to develop and display learning that reflects the intended outcomes of the instruction ...*

Impact is a transient thing; as we know, it completes the triangle alongside intent and implementation, but it has wider-reaching implications. A conversation with anyone about impact should not be data focused – it should be about the *substance* of education, treating teachers as experts in their domain as opposed to as data managers or crunchers of numbers. Yes, there is always a focus on achievement and measures of progress, but they mustn't dominate the dialogue. Instead, the dialogue that you can prepare for –in your line management meetings, performance reviews or just in professional conversation – should be what is taught and why – the need for autonomy as opposed to compliance. A discussion about curriculum impact when considered in conjunction with intent and implementation can be very liberating. Whereas intent is often general, you should see that implementation is – at nano/classroom level – unique to you. The impact of this therefore becomes the validation of your chosen approach and pedagogical principles; everything you do that is successful shapes the next iteration of the curriculum, or the next steps on the pupils' journey to the retention of knowledge.

Reflective task ◀◀◀

- How do you currently assess the impact of your teaching in your classroom and for your class(es)?

- What measures do you use and why?

It is important to consider not just what it tells you, but what it suggests, what actions it may stimulate and, perhaps most significantly, why that particular data set is being measured.

Now what? ◀◀◀

The desired impacts of a curriculum are more than just the raw data – so much more. For example, you might desire the following.

» *Teacher ownership and self-efficacy* – a happy teacher is an effective teacher, and an effective teacher improves student outcomes.

» *Attitudes to learning in students* – are pupils more ready, willing and able to learn? Do they feel happy and supported in their learning and in their classrooms? There is no more powerful and insightful tool than pupil voice, so use it.

» *Collaborative and supportive professional environments* – these are a clear indication of the open-door nature of classroom teaching supported by effective and worthwhile collaboration, sharing of good practice, communities of teaching and learning, and development of expertise and practice wisdom.

» *Powerful classrooms, with pupils working hard and learning well* – teachers maximise pupils' opportunities to learn and in doing so regularly activate deep thinking; pupils are not afraid to think critically, challenge their own thoughts and those of their peers, and develop a love of learning.

» *Rich and enriching wider school environments, with the achievements of pupils celebrated* – displays are regularly updated, pupils are publicly praised, the wider community is involved.

» *Development of new and innovative pedagogies built on research and evidence, both theoretical and practical* – a genuine open-door culture with no fear of judgement.

» *Teachers and leaders with a greater understanding of how students learn, and what environments support that experience.*

» *School-wide changes to policy and, more importantly, practice* – greater consistency grown out of deeper understanding and clarity. I have always believed that, in order to have everyone on the same page, the number of pages necessary to lay out guidance should be limited – keep it simple, keep it true; the fewer the instructions, the better the systems will be.

Assessing impact is a form of evaluation of the curriculum and its implementation; however, it is not an indicator of worth or value of the curriculum content, simply a summative measure of how well what was intended has been delivered:

> *an approach to evaluation which restricts itself to a concern with the assessment of pupil performance, while it may tell us much about the effectiveness of schools and teachers in 'delivering' the National Curriculum, will offer no evidence at all which might have a bearing on whether that curriculum is worth 'delivering' or, indeed, about whether the attainment targets set for the assessment programme are reasonable, let alone valuable.*
>
> (Kelly, 2004, p 148)

An impact is a cause that must have a resulting effect; you must then ask what will be done next to consolidate, build or repair? You must seek to understand the impact of your work, not just know the facts; like learners, you must accommodate and assimilate new knowledge into your existing schema for teaching and curriculum portrayal.

Reflective task ◀◀◀

Impact is therefore assessed not only through externally verified data, but also through pupil workbooks, and pupil voice and feedback.

- Are your assessment systems not only evident but also effective?

- How is this effectiveness facilitated?

- Are targets set using the language of the curriculum and with reference to its goals?

Practical task for tomorrow ◀◀◀

Short-term impact is measured through pupils' work in the classroom – your classroom.

- At the end of a lesson tomorrow, collect and review pupils' workbooks and consider whether or not the work you intended them to complete – and the concepts you wanted to them to learn – are appropriately manifested where pen has been set to paper.

- If not, consider your next steps – go back to the lesson plan and adapt it for teaching again so impact will be more noticeable.

Practical task for next week ◀◀◀

Impact is not just quantitative: it can be fleeting, transient, granular or glacial – but certainly never simple.

- To develop your practice, focus on the impact in terms of what worked for individual pupils, viewing your teaching through a lens of positivity; for every lesson or session you lead during the week, keep note of an impact. What was it? Why was it? Who was it?

Group	Who?	What?	Why?
Year 7 history	S A Mple	Verbal response to group discussion about causes of World War 1	S is normally reticent to comment; clearly he was confident, developed through feeling secure in the learning environment

Practical task for the longer term

You are the cause – the impact is the effect your teaching, your curation and presentation of the curriculum, and your pastoral support are having on your pupils. A good curriculum is rewarding to teach, so is good for your own health and well-being, often through a noticeable impact on your workload.

- As you plan individual lessons over the course of the next weeks and months, keep track of how long it takes to plan, design supporting resources, mark and give feedback on the content you teach; as you grow in confidence and develop your subject knowledge, you should see clear changes.

What next?

Further reading

Blatchford, R (ed) (2019) *The Primary Curriculum Leader's Handbook*. Woodbridge: John Catt Educational. This text elaborates further on curriculum impact.

References

Brophy, J (2000) *Teaching: Educational Practice Series 1*. Geneva: UNESCO IBE.

Deng, Z (2022) Powerful Knowledge, Educational Potential and Knowledge-rich Curriculum: Pushing the Boundaries. *Journal of Curriculum Studies*, 54(5): 599–617.

Kelly, A (2004) *The Curriculum: Theory and Practice* (5th ed). London: Sage.

Ofsted (2018) *An Investigation into How to Assess the Quality of Education Through Curriculum Intent, Implementation and Impact*. [online] Available at: https://assets.publish ing.service.gov.uk/government/uploads/system/uploads/attachment_data/file/936097/ Curriculum_research_How_to_assess_intent_and_implementation_of_curriculum_191218. pdf (accessed 14 February 2023).

Ofsted (2022) *Education Inspection Framework*. [online] Available at: www.gov.uk/ government/publications/education-inspection-framework/education-inspection-framework (accessed 19 March 2023).

Chapter 10   Evaluating the curriculum: next steps

What? (The big idea)

According to Engelmann and Carnine (2016, p v), 'A proper curriculum scrupulously details both the order of things that are to be taught and the requirements for adequate or appropriate teaching.' There are a lot of interplaying concepts here. What is scrupulous detail at each level? On what basis is the order of 'things that are to be taught' determined? What are the measures or benchmarks for adequate or appropriate teaching? In essence, this is the very challenge and thrill of curriculum development in any subject or phase – it is never dormant. The best curriculum development is cyclical, with evaluation at each stage and continued formative assessment that provides evidence to support responsiveness.

A seemingly standard 'display' of a curriculum sequence is the ubiquitous road map – a nicely designed graphic detailing the main concepts and topics taught at points across each academic year, providing a general overview of the 'journey' on which pupils embark across that stage of their education. However, this map – however well-crafted and aesthetically pleasing it may be – is only as ever as good as the learning pupils take from the journey: how much knowledge is acquired, retained and reused in a range of scenarios. Curricula often have 'pillars', a metaphor for the strong conceptual foundations on which learning is built; again, metaphors work but they are only figurative, not reality – the nicest acronym or most apposite architectural choice can be undone or knocked down very quickly if its aims are not manifested in clear pupil development.

So what?

Curriculum evaluation is a process used to gauge the effectiveness and value of the activities undertaken within the curriculum, We mustn't conflate assessment used to track pupils' progress through a prescribed curriculum as assessment of the quality of the curriculum overall; assessment validates how well the curriculum has been taught, but it does not validate the content choices of the taught curriculum.

Mary Kennedy (2016, p 6) suggests that teaching can be viewed as a set of five persistent problems, 'each of which presents a difficult challenge to teachers'.

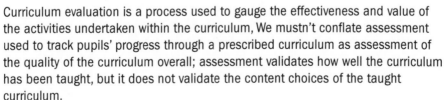

The first of these is *'portraying the curriculum'*. We have already debated the terminology used to describe how the intent of the curriculum manifests in classrooms – Kennedy (2016, p 10) suggests that teachers face the challenge of 'portraying' curriculum content in a way that *'makes it comprehensible to naïve minds'*. Curriculum content resides inert in the aforementioned road maps, the long- and medium-term plans, the specifications; by contrast, curriculum portrayals are active, given life by teachers' pedagogical choices and pupil responses. Kennedy argues that this portrayal begins before pupils arrive – when planning decisions about sequence and content portions are made – and then exists each day in real time and in real spaces. Classrooms are active, powerful spaces that can't always be predicted. She suggests that an individual lesson plan is simply a strategy tool for curriculum enactment, for converting passive to active.

Adopting this viewpoint asks you to question immediately what you are evaluating when you reflect on the success (or not) of your curriculum – did the impact justify the implementation, which in turn validated the intent? Or did it all go wrong and do you need to start again?

In evaluating the curriculum, you need to acknowledge that you are engaging in a process that endeavours to make learning experiences and the process of education relate better to individual pupils.

Teachers can evaluate against two clear aspects: merit and worth. Merit is the intrinsic value; it is implicit, inherent and independent, established without reference to a context. Worth is the value of an entity in reference to a particular context or subject domain. For example, a secondary English curriculum may have a great deal of merit in the eyes of the subject specialists teaching it – great text choices, rich in diversity, themes and theory – but has little worth for a primary teacher working with low-fluency English as an Additional Language (EAL) pupils. Some elements of specific curricula might require pedagogies that the teacher has not mastered and learning materials that the pupils cannot read. Therefore, curriculum evaluation should be concerned with assessing both merit and worth.

One essential element of any process of evaluation is leadership; evaluation of any value doesn't just happen, nor does it function in an environment absent of humility – if teachers aren't prepared to acknowledge that they could improve, what is the point in looking for places where they might improve? Henry Eyring (1998) puts it nicely: the best place to look for small change is in the things we do most often. What do you do most often? You teach. So the best place to start your process of curriculum evaluation is with your own teaching, where you are the leader of classroom instruction.

The key from the outset is an awareness of why you are evaluating, what you are looking for and – most importantly – what you will be prepared to do differently. Teachers mustn't make the mistake of using evaluation as a biased tool designed solely to justify their practice for the purposes of accountability; they should be using evaluation as a tool for improvement. As a classroom teacher, you can use evaluation to inform your reflections on your own teaching. How effective was your instruction in terms of implementing the intended curriculum? How can you determine the merit and worth of the curriculum?

Bradley's effectiveness model

Bradley's (1985) model uses ten key indicators that can be used to measure the effectiveness of the curriculum, for which the evaluator just has to decide 'yes' or 'no' in terms of the indicator's description.

Table 10.1 Indicators of effective curriculum development, adapted from Bradley, 1985

Indicator	Description
Vertical curriculum continuity	The course of study reflects a format that enables teachers to have quick and constant access to what is being taught in previous and subsequent years/key stages, following a spiral model.
Horizontal curriculum continuity	The course of study provides content and objectives that are common to all classrooms in each year group; daily lesson plans reflect the commonality across the year group.
Instruction based on curriculum	Lesson plans are derived from the course of study, and curriculum materials used correlate with the content and objectives; authentic and valuable tasks are developed.
Curriculum priority	Commitments are evident – both philosophical and financial; planning is supported through budget and time, and curriculum matters are prioritised in meetings.
Broad involvement	The local community and those in leadership are apprised of and approve the course of study.
Long-range planning	Each element of the wider curriculum is planned across a longer-term sequence and reviewed on a regular basis.
Decision-making clarity	Controversies or issues that arise during the development of the curriculum centre on the nature of the decision, not the person or persons who make it.

Indicator	Description
Positive human relations	Initial thoughts about the curriculum come from teachers and department leaders; all those participating in curriculum design are not afraid to disagree with each other, but communication lines remain strong and stable.
Theory-into-practice approach	All elements of the course of study are consistent, recognisable and authentic.
Planned change	Evidence shows that the planned curriculum is accepted by all, but also that the process of developing the curriculum is not a case of how to do it but a case of how to do it better.

With the Bradley model, if any of the ten indicators is identified as a 'no', those evaluating the curriculum should consider how to turn it into a 'yes'.

The evaluation process is the clearest example of why it is vital that all those involved in the portrayal of the curriculum are aware of the principles and values on which the curriculum design is based and its intentions have been sculpted; it is very difficult to evaluate the effectiveness of something without being aware of what it was intended to achieve and why the chosen approach was selected above others. This reminds you, as a classroom practitioner, of the importance of knowing not just 'what', but 'why'; evaluation is a further lever to avoid the trap of simple compliance.

The quality of the chosen evaluation model will have a significant impact on the quality of the evaluation itself – the process of evaluation needs to be understood, and in curriculum terms this means that those conducting the evaluation need a knowledge not only of the overall curriculum aims but also the instructional strategies used to portray them.

A good model for evaluating an effective curriculum will consider the following.

» The process can be implemented without excessive demands on resources.

» The model can be applied to all curriculum levels.

» The model makes provision for assessing all significant curriculum aspects.

» A useful distinction is made between the merit (intrinsic value) and worth (value for the given context).

» The model will be goal-oriented, emphasising objectives and outcomes.

» The model will be sensitive to the assessment of unintended effects, and therefore be responsive.

» It will be sensitive to and make provision for the unique contexts of the curriculum.

» It will consider the qualitative as well as quantitative aspects of the curriculum, not just be reliant on raw data.

When setting the goals and indicators around which the evaluation of effectiveness will be determined, it is important that the assessment process is linked back to the original vision, the objectives – these become the language of the evaluation. It is also key to ensure that the correct target populations are identified for each aspect of the evaluation, and that these contexts are considered carefully – for example, an excellent evaluative tool is pupil voice in terms of eliciting qualitative data from those in receipt of the curriculum, but it must be noted that the views of pupils are expressed in their own terms, not necessarily in the language of the curriculum intent agreed by those that designed it initially.

Reflective task ◀◀◀

Managing any evaluation entails addressing the following.

- What is the purpose and focus of the evaluation?

- What criteria are being used to make judgements?

- What evidence is to be collected, in what format, using which methods?

- Which stakeholders will be consulted?

- Who is responsible for the evaluation and who is accountable for the judgements made?

- What timescale and resources will be allocated?

- What action is to be taken as a result of the findings?

The last point there is the key – evaluation isn't just a compliance activity, showing that it is taking place, it is a formative activity, leading to improvement.

- Answer the questions above using your own teaching of a unit or scheme of work as the basis of the evaluation. What actions will you be taking?

Now what? ◀ ◀ ◀

Evaluation is used to provide the evidence that informs decision-making – it helps us answer the question 'Is what we are doing worthwhile?' We can break our evaluation into three dimensions:

1. the intended curriculum (intent – what is planned);

2. the offered curriculum (implementation – what you teach);

3. the received curriculum (impact – what pupils experience).

At classroom level, you can use a model to evaluate your own development as a practitioner, perhaps similar to the one proposed by Thomas Guskey (2000), who used five levels of data to evaluate professional learning. You can adapt it to evaluate your own classroom effectiveness.

» *Level 1: participants' reactions* – as the teacher, you are the participant in this case. As you portrayed the curriculum to your pupils, did you feel satisfied?

» *Level 2: participants' learning* – as well as enjoying the portrayal of the curriculum, did you learn anything new from it?

» *Level 3: organisational support and change* – did the way the curriculum was organised and the resources designed to support it play any part in its successful implementation?

» *Level 4: participants' use of new knowledge and skills* – did the experience of portraying the curriculum make a difference in your professional practice as a teacher?

» *Level 5: pupil outcomes* – the bottom line in education. Did pupils improve, learn more and meet their targets?

The act of portraying the curriculum and the data you elicit to assess its impact is part of a wider cycle of continued improvement, taking the evidence and putting it to work; if change is necessary, that change has to be clearly identified and the change sustained. Sharples et al (2018) suggest an implementation cycle of *'explore, prepare, deliver, sustain'*; it must be seen as a process, not an event.

Ongoing quality monitoring of curriculum is essential to ensure that the process is valid; different schools will devise different methods for this monitoring, but it can be assumed that one broadly used method is lesson observation, and perhaps the connection of this to performance management processes. Evaluation is largely concerned with values and judgements, which can sometimes lead to tensions, but if the process is open and the criteria are clear, then schools can create communities of enquiry, providing a climate of enquiry into and reflection on practice where evaluation is not a one-off or threatening activity, but instead is seen as part of a routine and a valuable part of professional life as a teacher. If there is a collaborative climate of trust and openness, then it is easier for individuals to successfully identify areas where they can improve, seek support from colleagues and make humble, sensible decisions in relation to curriculum, and ultimately the outcomes for pupils.

Good curriculum evaluation recognises the wealth of values and interests from all stakeholders, and leads to enhanced teaching and learning interactions, professional development and teacher improvement as a community, as opposed to a top-down activity where teachers feel curriculum is 'done to' them. Another benefit of this community evaluation is that it will engender stronger systems of professional development, where evidence-informed mechanisms allow for the design and implementation of a programme of teacher education that supports and enhances curriculum portrayal.

Successful evaluation will also acknowledge the factors of workload and well-being in teachers; too often, the curriculum and the need to 'cover all the content' become the biggest stick in the bundle with which teachers beat themselves. A good curriculum, where intent is clear, implementation is supported appropriately, impact is positive and monitoring is collaborative, will have a positive impact on the workload and therefore the well-being of those portraying it, manifesting it in classrooms.

The need for dialogue

Ultimately, in order for curriculum to be successful, there needs to be dialogue; everything on paper is just words until it is effectively realised in classrooms, and that realisation is purely reactionary unless it is built on firm foundations of intent – in essence, we must bridge the gap between theory and practice. Paulo Freire (1998, p 30) expresses this well:

> *Critical reflection on practice is a requirement of the relationship between theory and practice. Otherwise theory becomes simply 'blah, blah, blah,' and practice, pure activism.*

Freire suggests that dialogue cannot happen in a climate of hopelessness, emphasising the requirements of the correct culture. Dialogue generates critical thinking, and critical thinking generates informed improvement of the curriculum offer – the best way to improve is to talk. The curriculum therefore becomes the shared language that all those involved in its portrayal use – it is the lowest common denominator for positive collaboration.

Practical task for tomorrow ◀◀◀

Evaluation is a vital process, but also an active one; without further action, evaluation is merely procedural, sterile; you need to use it to stimulate and generate targets. After you finish your last lesson tomorrow, set aside some time to reflect; how successfully did I portray the curriculum today? How do I know?

- *What?* What happened, what did I do?

- *So what?* Why is that important? What was the result?

- *Now what?* What do I need to do differently next time to avoid the same result?

Practical task for next week ◀◀◀

Evaluation is about being prepared to make changes where opportunity has been identified; however, there are always opportunity costs involved in any form of change, as making the amendments takes time, which often comes from somewhere else, so there needs to be a justifiable trade-off – is this the right change to make?

Evaluation also strengthens anticipation; regular review breeds capacity to predict issues and to be proactive in mitigating them.

- Look ahead to your next topic for teaching. What potential issues can you foresee?

- How can you pre-mortem and put something in place to prevent those issues happening, as in the example below?

Topic of study: GCSE English Language Paper 2	
Potential issue	**Mitigation**
Nineteenth-century non-fiction element; pupils unfamiliar with language and style	Begin exposure to nineteenth-century texts early so there is familiarity – approach texts from a thematic as opposed to technical perspective to forge more relevant connections.

Practical task for the longer term ◀◀◀

Part of developing our self-efficacy in curriculum portrayal is noticing our own professional development.

- As you deliver material to your pupils, keep a regular track of any time when you use a new skill, a new pedagogy or new resource.

- Why did you introduce it?

- What effect did it have?

- Was it better than that which was already in place?

Never forget that you are at the centre of your own teacher growth; by aligning your own professional development with your understanding of the curriculum you are responsible for portraying, you will help improve not only your own confidence and competence, but also the outcomes for your students. Curriculum is a living thing; it needs nurturing, and it needs listening to. Never be afraid to adapt or innovate in the space you provide for yourself through effective and efficient practice.

What next? ◀◀ ◀

Further reading

Numerous useful articles and reflections on curriculum can be found through the Chartered College and its *Impact* journal: https://impact.chartered.college/issue/issue-4-designing-a-curriculum (accessed 12 February 2023).

References

Bradley, L (1985) *Curriculum Leadership and Development Handbook*. Englewood Cliffs, NJ: Prentice-Hall.

Engelmann, S and Carnine, D (2016) *Theory of Instruction: Principles and Applications*. Eugene, OR: NIFDI Press.

Eyring, H (1998) *The Lord Will Multiply the Harvest*. [online] Available at: www.churchofjesuschrist.org/study/manual/teaching-seminary-preservice-readings-religion-370-471-and-475/the-lord-will-multiply-the-harvest?lang=eng (accessed 6 April 2023).

Freire, P (1998) *Pedagogy of Freedom: Ethics, Democracy, and Civic Courage*. Lanham, MD: Rowman & Littlefield.

Guskey, T R (2000) *Evaluating Professional Development.* Thousand Oaks, CA: Corwin Press.

Kennedy, M (2016) Parsing the Practice of Teaching. *Journal of Teacher Education*, 67(1): 6–17.

Sharples, J, Albers, B and Fraser, S (2018) *Putting Evidence to Work: A School's Guide to Implementation*. London: Education Endowment Foundation.

Acronym buster

Acronym	What does it stand for?	Notes/links
AfL	assessment for learning	
BTEC	Business and Technology Education Council award	
CPD	continuing professional development	
DfE	Department for Education	
EAL	English as an Additional Language	
EBE	evidence-based education	https://evidencebased.education/
ECF	Early Career Framework	https://assets.publishing.service.gov.uk/government/uploads/system/uploads/attachment_data/file/978358/Early-Career_Framework_April_2021.pdf
ECT	early career teacher	
ECT mentor	early career teacher mentor	
EEF	Education Endowment Foundation	https://educationendowmentfoundation.org.uk
GCSE	General Certificate of Secondary Education	
ITT(E)	Initial Teacher Training (Education)	
MAT	multi-academy trust	

Acronym	What does it stand for?	Notes/links
NC	national curriculum	www.gov.uk/government/collections/national-curriculum
Ofsted	Office for Standards in Education, Children's Services and Skills	
PCK	pedagogical content knowledge	
QTS	qualified teacher status	

Index

Note: Page numbers in **bold** and *italics* denote tables and figures, respectively.